The Truth About College

OTHER BOOKS BY SCOTT EDELSTEIN

College: A User's Manual (Bantam)
Surviving Freshman Composition (Lyle Stuart)
The Indispensable Writer's Guide (HarperCollins)
Putting Your Kids Through College (Consumer Reports Books)
The No-Experience-Necessary Writer's Course (Scarborough House)
Manuscript Submission (Writer's Digest Books)
The Writer's Book of Checklists (Writer's Digest Books)

The Truth About
COLLEGE
How to Survive and Succeed
as a Student in the Nineties

by Scott Edelstein

A Lyle Stuart Book
Published by Carol Publishing Group

A Lyle Stuart Book
Published by Carol Publishing Group
Lyle Stuart is a registered trademark of Carol Communications, Inc.

Editorial Offices: 600 Madison Avenue, New York, N.Y. 10022
Sales & Distribution Offices: 120 Enterprise Avenue, Secaucus, N.J. 07094
In Canada: Musson Book Company, a division of General Publishing Co., Ltd., Don Mills, Ontario

Queries regarding rights and permissions should be addressed to Carol Publishing Group, 120 Enterprise Avenue, Secaucus, N.J. 07094

Carol Publishing Group books are available at special discounts for bulk purchases, sales promotions, fund-raising, or educational purposes. Special editions can be created to specifications. For details contact: Special Sales Department, Carol Publishing Group, 120 Enterprise Avenue, Secaucus, N.J. 07094

Manufactured in the United States of America
10 9 8 7 6 5 4 3 2 1

Library of Congress Cataloging-in-Publication Data

Edelstein, Scott
     The truth about college : how to succeed as a student
in the nineties / by Scott Edelstein.
          p.   cm.
     "A Lyle Stuart book."
     ISBN 0-8184-0546-5
          1. College student orientation--United States. 2. Study, Method
of. I. Title
LB2343.32.E36   1991
378.1'98—dc20   91-10650
                                                      CIP

To Barbara

Contents

Introduction   Why This Book Is Different—and Essential   ix

An Important Note on Titles   xi

1. Applying and Getting In   1
2. Financial Aid   22
3. Registration and Scheduling   54
4. Rules and Regulations   70
5. Parking and Transportation   81
6. Advisors   86
7. Teachers   93
8. Administrators and Staff   116
9. Classes and Other Forms of Learning   120
10. Papers   132
11. Tests and Exams   139
12. Grades   147
13. Graduation Requirements   154
14. Housing and Food   166
15. Campus Facilities   180
16. Other Students   187
17. What You'll Learn in College   197
18. The Value of Your Education (and Your Degree)   200
19. Staying Sane   205
20. The Pleasures and Rewards of College   219

Why This Book Is
Different—and Essential

The Truth About College is unlike any other book ever written about college. It's not a collection of well-meaning but banal advice such as, "Outline your papers before you write them," or "Don't wait until the last minute to study for exams." There are already plenty of books full of these kinds of educational clichés and rah-rah motivational techniques.

This book is different. It's a survival manual. It's based not on what colleges should be or pretend to be, but on what they actually are, do, and will demand of you in the 1990s. And much of *The Truth About College* is based on what colleges do wrong, and on what they may do *to* you in their worst moments.

College can be an exciting, wonderful, and very gratifying place. But it can also be frustrating, confusing, or just plain agonizing. You may find yourself with some instructors who can't teach, and some who can't even speak English clearly; with an advisor who gives bad or incorrect advice; with a financial aid office that gives you less aid than you genuinely need; with registration procedures that require you to wait in line for hours, only to be told that the classes you want are filled; with monolithic dorms that look and feel like prisons; with computer errors in billing or scheduling that no one seems to be able to fix; or with administrators who treat you like a product on an assembly line.

If you're a college student, or planning to become one, you should know that your school will probably throw at least some of these problems at you, and very likely others as well. In fact, some of these dilemmas may already be quite familiar to you.

The Truth About College will help you to anticipate dozens of common problems that might come your way in college. It will give you clear, specific, step-by-step directions for solving and/or coping with each one. More important, this book will show you exactly what you can do to *avoid* most of these potential problems and keep them from landing in your lap.

In short, *The Truth About College* will enable you to be an intelligent educational consumer. It will tell you what to do if a teacher singles you out for ridicule or harassment. It will show you how to convince a financial aid office to improve an inadequate aid package. It will explain how to get out of taking unnecessary prerequisites. It will tell you what to do to get an unfair grade changed. And it will give you specific steps and strategies for dealing successfully with a great many other college-related problems.

What qualifies me to write this book? How do I know about all the dilemmas that colleges thrust upon students—*and* how to avoid them, solve them, or deal with them?

I know because I've taught college for more than a decade, and have worked with over a thousand students from a wide variety of backgrounds. I've taught at colleges of all types and sizes, from state universities to community colleges to a liberal arts school. Besides teaching in the classroom, I've been a college-level tutor and an advisor.

I know what goes on behind the scenes in college offices and administrations because I've worked as an intern for the provost of Oberlin College.

And I know what students go through because I'm still a student myself. I'm currently working on a Ph.D. in English from the State University of New York at Buffalo.

The Truth About College will provide you with all the insights and inside information you need to become a successful student—and to keep college from interfering with your education.

Scott Edelstein
Minneapolis, Minnesota

An Important Note on Titles

People who work in colleges and universities, and the offices they work in, go by a variety of unusual titles. Below are the most common of these titles, their definitions, and the most frequently used synonyms for each. I will refer to some of these people and offices frequently.

For the sake of consistency, I will use only the titles in the left-hand column in this book. However, the synonymous titles are also widely used, so please take note of them.

Campus Police A private police force which enforces college rules on campus. It is operated by the college and normally has no power or jurisdiction outside the campus. At most schools, the campus police function as both security officers and traffic patrolmen; some large universities, however, have two separate units, one for security and another for traffic control and parking enforcement. *Also known as: Security, Campus Security*

Dean A powerful administrator in charge of a wide range of college functions and services. Most colleges have several, or more than several, different deans: one in charge of academics, one in charge of student activities, one in charge of admissions, and so on. Some colleges have a dean of men and a dean of women; some have a special dean of minority affairs. The deans know the rules, often make them, and have the authority to bend them. They are your best and most powerful on-campus advocates in most situations, and they are the people to complain to and turn to for help when a teacher, staffperson, or other administrator is harming you or failing to help you. Most colleges also have several assistant and associate deans, who can also serve as your advocates.

Dean of Academic Affairs The person in charge of all courses and academic programs at a college.
Also known as: Dean of the College
Note: Instead of one dean of academic affairs, most large universities have several different deans, one for each college or school within the university. For instance, there might be a dean of the college of arts and sciences, a dean of the college of nursing, a dean of the graduate school, a dean of the school of architecture, and so on.

Dean of Students The person in charge of all student support services, including housing, dining, counseling, transportation, etc.
Also known as: Dean of Student Affairs, Dean of Student Life, Dean of Student Activities
Note: Large universities sometimes have separate deans of housing and/or dining, counseling, etc.

Department Head The director of an individual academic department (such as chemistry, sociology, art, etc.). A department head usually serves as both the chief administrator for the department and a part-time instructor, though at very large universities some department heads are full-time administrators. Department heads have the power to bend some department policies and rules.
Also known as: Department Chair, Department Chairman, Department Chairperson

Provost The chief academic officer; the person at a college or university who is in charge of everything directly connected with learning and education, including all course offerings, all academic departments, all off-campus programs, the library, and the entire faculty. The dean of academic affairs usually reports directly to the provost.

Also known as: Academic Vice President, Vice President for Academic Affairs

Note: Some large universities often have more than one provost— usually one for each college or academic unit. They may also have an array of associate provosts, vice provosts, etc.

Registration   The office in charge of course registration, academic records, and transcripts. Sometimes the person in charge of this office is called the *registrar.*

Also known as: Registration and Records, Registrar's Office

Note: At some schools, the registration, records, and/or transcript offices may be separate.

Treasurer   The person in charge of all of a college's financial matters, including billing and student accounts.

Also known as: Bursar

"Never let the university interfere with your education."

—GEORGE BERNARD SHAW, to his nephew

1

Applying and Getting In

Despite what some people claim, colleges are not all begging for students. Some schools (and not just the most selective ones) are turning away more applicants than ever.

At the most selective colleges and universities, competition for admission is at least as tough as usual—and, at some schools, even tougher. Competition has also increased in recent years at many moderately selective colleges, including quite a few state schools. Some of these colleges are turning away record numbers of applicants.

It's true that some private colleges with low or no admission standards are having trouble filling their freshman classes. But at many community colleges, and many state universities with minimal admission requirements, applications are at an all-time high. Some state schools are filling up their freshman classes by March or April, and turning away hundreds or even thousands of applicants simply for lack of room.

Solution: Apply to colleges early. If you plan to begin school next fall, get all your applications in the mail by January 10—or even earlier, under any of the following circumstances:

• Some of the most selective colleges (Harvard, Williams, Stanford, etc.) have application deadlines as early as January 1 or December 15. Be sure to meet or beat any deadline.

• If you're applying to a college outside of the country in which

1

you live, mail your application by January 5—or send it via overnight mail.

• If you apply for Early Decision or Early Action admission (in which you request an early response from your first-choice college), submit your application by the school's deadline, which may be as early as November 1.

• If you apply for midyear admission, get your application in by the deadline, which might be as early as October 1.

Take all your college applications quite seriously. Allow yourself plenty of time to respond thoughtfully and thoroughly to each question—particularly each essay question. Photocopy each application, and, for your first draft, fill in the photocopy. As necessary, carefully rewrite, edit, and proofread each response. When you've got the best finished product you can produce, neatly type all your responses on the actual application. If you are not a good typist, have someone who is do the typing for you.

College catalogs, viewbooks, and admissions representatives will not always give you a thorough, clear, or realistic picture of the schools they represent.

Admissions representatives and college catalogs can provide you with plenty of good information about schools. But, since part of their job is to attract new students, all of the information they give you is going to have a positive spin to it.

Viewbooks—introductory pamphlets put out by many liberal arts colleges and universities, particularly the more selective ones—are even more overt pieces of public relations. Typically, these publications are lavishly prepared, full of gorgeous color photographs of the campus, and peppered with enthusiastic quotes from students and/or instructors. Viewbooks invariably paint extremely rosy pictures of the colleges they introduce. These pictures are far from complete.

College catalogs (and sometimes viewbooks) can also create a misleading impression of what course offerings are available. Normally a catalog will list any course which the college has offered at least once in the past two to four years—even if that course is taught only twice per decade. Thus a college catalog might list, say, fifteen different sociology courses, but the sociology department might offer only three or four courses each term.

Catalogs of community and junior colleges are especially likely to misrepresent what courses are normally available. For example, during a typical term, the English department of a community college might offer a total of only five courses: eighty sections of Freshman Composition 1, forty-five sections of Freshman Composition 2, a section of business writing, and two literature classes. Yet the catalog might list no less than twenty-five English courses: two in composition, three in other types of writing, and twenty in literature. The three writing and twenty literature courses are rotated each term.

Solution: Don't make a decision on any college based on its viewbook, its catalog, and/or what an admissions rep tells you. These will give you a biased and incomplete view.

The only way to truly get a feel for what a school is like is to visit it yourself. I *strongly* urge you to visit any college or university you are seriously thinking of attending before deciding where to enroll— and, ideally, before you apply for admission. See the section below for more details.

To get a list of the courses a college actually offers, call its registration office and ask to be sent the class schedule for the current term (or the upcoming term, if it's available).

If a college does not offer the range of courses you want, think seriously about attending a different school; or else plan to supplement its course offerings with independent studies, internships, and/or courses taken at other colleges.

If you do not visit a college before enrolling in it, you may end up being miserable once you get there.

Would you rent a room or apartment without first looking it over? Would you buy a car without first test-driving it? Would you marry someone without first meeting him or her? The obvious answer to all of these questions is no. Yet many (too many) students decide which college to attend before they ever set foot on campus.

Some students get lucky, and wind up liking the school they choose. But others find themselves dissatisfied with their courses, their teachers, their fellow students, and/or the overall campus atmosphere. Often they transfer to other colleges—or drop out of school entirely.

You will probably spend two to five years—perhaps longer—in college. Why not make an informed choice, so that these years can be as useful, as educational, and as enjoyable as possible? A little time, effort, and money invested in some firsthand research can pay enormous rewards.

Solution: As you research colleges, you'll find yourself most interested in a few (perhaps three to eight) schools. These might all seem similar on the surface—for example, they might all be liberal arts colleges—but I promise you that they will be very different. Even those schools with very similar academic programs may have very different social and intellectual atmospheres.

Try to visit every one of these schools before you must choose which college to attend. If this is out of the question, visit as many as you can. A day or two on campus can give you a real taste of what life at that college will be like—and it will tell you far more than any catalog, viewbook, admissions representative, or recent graduate can.

Except under highly unusual circumstances, *do not accept admission from any college that you have not yet visited.* If you must choose between two or three schools, don't make a decision until you have visited them all. This can save you a great deal of difficulty and heartache later.

To get the most out of any campus visit, follow these guidelines:

First of all, go alone, not with your parents. Virtually everyone—teachers, administrators, and other students—will treat you differently when you're with your parents than when you're alone. If your parents are dead set against your visiting colleges on your own, or if the thought of going alone terrifies you, a good compromise is to make an initial visit with your parents, then return on your own before deciding where to enroll.

Plan each campus visit several weeks in advance. The ideal length of time for a visit is about thirty-six to forty-eight hours—long enough to get a feel for things, to sit in on a couple of classes, to eat several meals on campus, and to stay overnight in a dormitory. If the college is in or very near your hometown, you may of course make several shorter visits instead; however, if you plan to live on campus, it is a very good idea to stay overnight in a dorm and eat a few dining-hall meals, so that you know exactly what dorm life will be like.

If possible, visit colleges on weekdays, when classes are in session and instructors are on campus. If you want to get a feel for both a typical weekday and a weekend, plan to arrive on a Thursday evening and leave on a Saturday. (Visiting during the week will mean missing a couple of days of high school. Go ahead and miss them; arrange with teachers in advance to get the assignments for the days you will be away. Have your parents write a note explaining where you will be and what you will be doing. If your attendance officer or any of your teachers won't excuse you during these days, take the unexcused absences. Your potential future gain will far outweigh any petty high school punishment.)

Avoid visiting campuses during the last two weeks of the term or during the week before midterm exams. During these times, students tend to be frazzled, extremely busy, and sometimes irritable. Also avoid visiting during the first two weeks of the term, when enthusiasm and energy are artificially high.

The best months of the year to visit colleges are October and November. Most schools are geared up for visitors then, and these are excellent months to do on-campus interviews; indeed, some of the most high-powered schools do no admissions interviews at all after November or December.

Once you've decided on some dates to visit a school—and a set of backup dates, just in case—call its admissions office. Say that you wish to arrange a campus visit and an admissions interview, and mention the dates that you have in mind. Ask if it is possible to spend a night in a dorm and eat in one or more of the campus dining halls. Also ask to get a tour of the campus.

When you arrive on campus, do the following:

• Walk around campus and get to know the layout. Does the campus seem reasonably attractive, safe, and comfortable?

• Visit the library and browse through its collection of books and magazines. Does it have a large enough collection? Does it have a good selection of materials in the subjects that most interest you? Does it have enough places to study, or are all of the study carrels taken? What are its hours?

- Visit the student center. What does it offer in the way of fun, food, and places to sit and talk? Is it comfortable? What are its hours?

- Go to the offices of the departments that most interest you. At each one, ask for a copy of the department handbook (if one is available) and/or for a list of courses offered by the department during the current term. If a list of next term's courses is available, get that, too. Look through this material carefully.

- If a particular course interests you, sit in on it. Arrive a few minutes early; explain to the teacher that you're thinking of applying to the college, and ask if you may observe the class. If the teacher says yes, stay for the whole class meeting; observe but do not participate unless you are asked or encouraged to. (If the teacher won't let you sit in, don't be offended. Teachers have the right to keep visitors out, and it doesn't mean they're unfair or unfriendly.)

Try to sit in on at least two different classes during your visit. Introductory classes are usually your best bets.

- Get a good look at some of the dorms. Are the common areas (lounges, bathrooms, etc.) reasonably clean and comfortable? Do they feel like pleasant places to live, or more like military compounds? If you can, get a peek into one of the rooms. Is it passably large and comfortable? If certain dorms are reserved for freshmen, visit at least one of these.

Since accommodations can vary widely from dorm to dorm, make a note of the three or four dorms that you like best; then, if and when you apply for on-campus housing, make these dorms your first choices.

- Eat in college dining halls. If the school has several different dining halls, eat in as many different ones as you can. This will give you a good idea what the food will be like and what options are available.

Don't be scared off by natural food or kosher dining halls. Their food is worth sampling, and often it is some of the best food on campus.

- Visit any other campus facility that especially interests you—the gym, the microcomputer lab, the language labs, etc. Note their hours.

• Talk to students. Ask them if they're basically happy or dissatisfied with the school. Find out what they feel are the college's biggest pluses and minuses. Ask if there are any teachers especially worth studying with—or especially worth avoiding.

• If particular teachers sound intriguing—because of either their reputations or the courses they teach—visit with them during their office hours. You can find out any instructor's office location and hours from the secretary in his or her department.

• Walk or drive around the town or neighborhood where the college is located. Does it seem lively or dead? Safe or dangerous? Note what shops and amusements are nearby. Where is the nearest post office, bank, copying center, grocery store, laundromat, drugstore, movie theater, etc.?

If the college is in a midsize or large city, you may wish to check out other parts of town as well.

• Get and read a copy of the local newspaper. If you are thinking of living off campus, look at the classified ads for apartments and rooms for rent to get an idea of what is available and how much it costs.

• Read the college paper, too. If an issue has been recently published, copies will be available all over campus.

• Take an official campus tour.

• Go on an admissions interview. See below for complete details on preparing for these interviews.

• If you like, attend one or two social events (dances, concerts, parties, poetry readings, etc.).

• At the end of your visit, ask yourself how you feel about the college. Did you like the students you met? Did you like the overall feel of the campus? Were you pleased with the courses and teachers? Trust your gut on this. A school that feels right probably *is* right for you; but a college that makes you feel uncomfortable is probably a college to avoid.

Even if a college does not require an admissions interview, students who do go for interviews may be more likely to be admitted than those who don't.

Just as the only real way to get a feel for a college is to visit it, the only real way the people in an admissions office can get a feel for who you are is to meet you and talk with you. Before your interview, you are just a name, an application form, and a series of numbers and responses; afterward you are a real person about whom an admissions committee can make an informed judgment. If an admissions officer gets to talk with you and likes the person he or she talks with, your chances for admission go up dramatically.

Very few colleges absolutely require an interview. However, the more selective a school is, the more important an interview is—and the more of a difference it can make in getting you admitted. (One exception is Stanford, which does no admissions interviews at all.)

Solution: Go on an admissions interview at every college which seriously interests you.

If possible, do your interview on campus, as part of your campus visit. Call the admissions office several weeks in advance to arrange a day and time.

Arrive at your interview on time. You should be well groomed and neatly dressed, but don't dress up as much as you would for a job interview. For a male, neatly pressed slacks and a sweater or sport coat are fine; a tie is optional. For a female, a conservative dress, or a nice skirt and blouse, is the norm. Wear little or no makeup and jewelry. People of both sexes should avoid anything loud, flashy, or overly formal (e.g., a business suit).

Otherwise, be yourself. The interview will focus mostly on you, so be ready to talk about yourself and your interests. *Don't* prepare stock answers, attempt to sound scholarly or intellectual, spout platitudes ("I want an education with both breadth and depth"), or try to say what you think the interviewer wants to hear. Admissions officers can smell bullshit a mile away.

Instead, you might talk about some of the unusual things you've done or are interested in. If you've designed, printed, and sold artsy T-shirts at street fairs, say so. If you've worked as a veterinarian's assistant, talk about that. If you've built your own guitar or flown an ultralight or run your own business, discuss that. Interviewers are most interested in what makes you unique. Assume that the interviewer wants to know who you are and what makes you different from the typical bright high school student. Also be prepared to explain what interests you most about the college.

A secondary purpose of any interview is for you to find out more about the college, so come prepared with three or four questions. For instance, you might ask, "How would you describe the general atmosphere here?" or "What, in your opinion, makes this college special or sets it apart from others?" Or you might simply ask, "What do you think is the college's greatest strength right now, and its greatest drawback for new students?" Also feel free to ask more specific questions about programs, courses, and departments.

Interviews typically run twenty to thirty minutes. If yours runs longer, that's fine—in fact, it's usually a good sign.

If you absolutely cannot do an on-campus interview, call the admissions office to find out if you can be interviewed by an admissions representative or alumnus in or near your hometown. Many schools send admissions people on multicity tours to promote their schools and interview prospective applicants; typically, these tours take place in October and November, though they can run as early as September or as late as February or March. Other schools offer interviews through nearby alumni. Alumni interviews can usually be scheduled for almost any time, though normally the earlier the better.

If even this arrangement is not possible, ask to schedule a telephone interview with an admissions officer at a mutually convenient time. Some colleges do phone interviews; some don't.

There are only three circumstances in which I do not recommend an admissions interview:

• If you are so shy that you cannot hold a conversation. (In this case, I urge you to consult a psychologist, who may be able to help you speak more freely and openly.)

• If a college will admit you *automatically* without an interview, as is the case at community colleges and many state universities. If a college is at all selective, however, set up an interview.

• If a school simply will not do interviews at all.

If any portion of your application is lost or fails to arrive, the college's admissions office will not process your application.

Most schools start an admissions file on you when the first part of your application (a letter of recommendation, test scores, your high school transcript, etc.) arrives. However, the admissions people will normally not review your application until they've received every item they need. If any one of these items is not sent or is lost—*even if it is lost by the admissions office*—your application will not be processed.

All of this is also true for financial aid applications and financial aid offices.

Solution: Get all materials in to admissions offices well in advance—by January 15 or three weeks before the deadline, whichever is earlier. Take any standardized tests (ACTs, SATs, Achievement Tests, etc.) early enough so that admissions offices receive the results by this time. Ask the people writing recommendations for you to get them in as soon as possible.

Two weeks before your deadline, call each admissions office and check to make sure that your application is complete. If it is not, immediately arrange to replace any missing items—and, to be safe, repeat this whole process one week before the deadline.

Your chances of getting into a school are based in part on factors having nothing to do with your academic record or intellectual potential. One of these factors may be family finances.

Although strict quotas are illegal, some schools try to strike a balance among their new students in terms of sex, race, and region or country. To attain this balance, an admissions office may skew its decisions in favor of certain groups.

Usually this is a matter of mathematics rather than bias, because it is based largely or entirely on who applies for admission. For example, if a college with a national reputation gets a flood of applications from the midwestern and eastern United States, but relatively few from the South, the southern applicants may have a slightly easier time getting in. If a school that enrolls about the same number of men and women students receives eight hundred applications from men but only 620 from women, a higher percentage of female applicants are going to be admitted. Another variation: Some state schools are required by law to admit a certain number or percentage of applicants from within the state; as a result, out-of-state applicants may have a tougher time getting admitted than in-state applicants.

At many colleges, a different kind of math plays a very important part in admissions decisions: financial accounting. Some schools admit students largely or entirely on their ability to pay tuition and fees, not on their intellectual promise. Other schools take both intellectual ability and finances into account; while these colleges strive to admit only the best applicants, sometimes they will reject a poor but brilliant student in favor of a well-heeled but less promising one.

This unfortunate situation never occurs at state or community colleges. Only certain private colleges, and by no means all of them, engage in this practice. You should also know that most—but not all—of the most selective private colleges make admissions decisions without regard for applicants' family finances.

Solution 1: Apply to at least one school that interests you where you will clearly be a cut above the great majority of applicants. Your qualifications will thus be strong enough to outweigh any financial or demographic considerations. If you're a first-rate student, pick a moderately selective school; if you're a good but not extraordinary student, pick a college that is only slightly selective. (If you're an average or poor student, pick a community college, or a state university in your home state that admits all or nearly all applicants.) This ensures that you have somewhere to go if demographics or finances work against you.

Solution 2: If, for whatever reason, the college you most want to attend turns you down, there are several back doors through which you may be able to enter:

(1) Enroll as a nondegree student, either in the college's regular program—or, if this is not possible, through its extension program (sometimes called continuing education, community education, the evening college, etc.). After you have completed two or more terms with good grades (a B average or higher), reapply for admission as a degree candidate. Chances are you'll be admitted; once you are admitted, the credits you earned should count toward your degree.

There is one drawback to this plan, however: Nondegree students are ineligible for many forms of financial aid.

(2) Some large universities have a special college or program that sets lower admissions standards. The University of Minnesota, for example, has a separate school called the General College. Call the admissions office to see if such a program or school exists, and, if so, how you can be admitted to it. After you have earned a B average for two or more terms, you can reapply for admission to the regular program, with good chances for success.

Some of these special schools and programs are open only to certain groups (e.g., minorities, single parents, people below certain income levels, people whose parents did not attend college, etc.).

(3) A few universities, such as Penn State and Ohio University, have branch campuses that set lower admissions standards. Attend one of these branch campuses for a year or more, then apply to transfer to the main campus.

(4) Go to college elsewhere for two terms or more. Work hard. Then reapply as a transfer student.

High grades (even straight A's) and high standardized test scores are not guarantees of admission at highly selective colleges.

The twenty or thirty most selective colleges on the continent— Yale, Columbia, Swarthmore, McGill, etc.—turn down far more applicants than they accept. Most of the applicants to these schools have excellent academic records. Admissions officers at these colleges therefore look well beyond mere numbers: They look at what makes each student unique or promising.

A student who has top grades and test scores, but who has done little or nothing except go to school, might be turned down by many of these colleges. However, a student with unexceptional grades and test scores who has a great deal of artistic talent, entrepreneurial ability, or simple eloquence and human insight might be granted admission.

Solution: When you fill out each college application, demonstrate what makes you unique or special. In your essays, discuss some of your most unusual interests or experiences (but only to the degree that they relate to the questions, of course). And don't rely on the standard application materials: Add one, or two, or several supplements. If you drove across Canada last summer and kept a journal, send a photocopy of the journal; if you've written several songs, record them and send a cassette; if you spent the summer working in a flower shop, send some photographs of floral arrangements you designed. Let the admissions people feel they're making a decision about *you*, not just a set of responses and statistics. If you have the grades, the test scores, *and* these supporting materials, you maximize your chances for admission.

And if you're talented and convincing enough, these additional materials can sometimes get you admitted to first-rate colleges even if your grades and test scores are mediocre or worse.

Your high school guidance counselor may offer you extremely bad advice about college.

There are some good guidance counselors out there. But there are also a great many ignorant, narrow-minded, and just plain dopey ones as well.

Guidance counselors *can* offer useful general advice and information. But when it comes to advising individual students or recommending particular colleges, many of them do more harm than good.

Solution: If a guidance counselor offers you specific advice on choosing a college, don't take it very seriously. Do your own research and draw your own conclusions.

Many colleges are located in dirty, ugly, and/or crime-ridden cities or neighborhoods.

In fact, there seems to be little relation between the quality of a college and the safety or beauty of the surrounding neighborhood. Some of the most humble schools are in clean, safe, elegant suburbs, while some highly rated schools (Case Western Reserve, Yale, Clark, etc.) border on slums.

Solution: When you visit campuses, tour the surrounding neighborhood on foot or by car. If it seems unsafe, unattractive, or both, this doesn't necessarily mean you shouldn't go to that school—but it does mean that if you do enroll, you will need to take precautions. Follow the guidelines on crime prevention and safety that begin on pages 184 and 193.

If the college is an island of relative safety in an otherwise doubtful neighborhood, seriously consider living on campus. Or, consider living some distance away—across town, in the next town, or in the nearby countryside—and driving or taking the bus to school.

Private college consultants are almost always expensive—sometimes very expensive—and some of their advice can be worthless, or even harmful.

College consultants offer advice, guidance, and moral support to college applicants and their parents. However, no credential, education, or training of any kind is required to become a college consultant, and the profession is currently completely unregulated.

Most of what college consultants have to say is helpful. But in one important area—choosing which colleges to apply to or which one to attend—their advice ranges from mildly useful at best to horribly misleading.

Solution: A college consultant is a luxury. If your parents feel strongly about hiring one, fine. But if they were to take the money they would spend on a college consultant and use it to pay for you to visit several colleges, they may be making a much wiser investment.

Furthermore, you and your parents can learn most or all of what a college consultant would teach you on your own, provided you're willing to do a little research. An excellent place for your parents to begin is one of my other books, *Putting Your Kids Through College* (Consumer Reports Books, 1989); a good place for you to begin is the book you are reading now.

If your parents do purchase the advice of a college consultant, listen carefully to what she says. If the information and guidance she gives you makes sense, follow it; if it doesn't, ignore it.

Do *not* apply to any college simply because a college consultant recommended it. Only you can decide which schools will suit you. If a consultant (or anyone else) suggests that you look into a certain college, feel free to do so—but don't stray from your strategy of doing your own research, visiting those schools that seem most promising *to you*, and making your own final decision based on firsthand experience.

Computerized college search services may steer you wrong.

A number of private organizations, as well as some high school guidance offices, now offer a computerized service that matches up students and colleges. This works a great deal like computer dating services, and it is roughly as effective: Sometimes it works and sometimes it doesn't.

To use this service, you fill out a form which asks for a good deal of simple information about you: your interests, grades, test scores, possible career plans, etc. The computer program then takes this information and finds you some colleges that, at least on paper, would appear to suit your needs and be reasonably likely to grant you admission.

These search services are usually not very expensive, but they are also not terribly reliable. Because they work only with simple, quantifiable pieces of information, they simply cannot address intangibles such as the intellectual and social climate of a college.

Solution: Don't rely on a computer chip to determine two to five years of your life. Do your own research into colleges; visit those schools that most interest you; then make your own best decision.

A college search service *can* be a useful tool in helping you establish an initial group of schools to research further. It may also let you know of some potentially appropriate colleges that you might otherwise have overlooked or never heard of.

Two tools that you may find at least as useful, and far less expensive, are *The College Planning Search Book* (1990; available for $6.00 postpaid from American College Testing Program, Box 168, Iowa City, IA 52243) and *College Match* by Steven R. Antonoff and Marie A. Friedemann (1991; available for $11.45 postpaid from Octameron Associates, Box 2748, Alexandria, VA 22301). Each of these volumes will take you through a step-by-step process for locating a group of colleges that may be right for you.

A college's prestige or reputation may mean little or nothing in terms of the quality of education it offers, or the value of the degrees it awards.

Virtually every college, from Harvard to Ohio State to your nearby community college, has its share of excellent teachers and classes. Every college also has its share of terrible and mediocre ones. If you take the time and trouble to choose your teachers and courses carefully, you can get a good to excellent education no matter where you go to school. See chapters 7 and 9 for complete details on selecting the best teachers and classes, and making sure that you get into those classes.

Most people overestimate the value of prestige. There are only five schools in the U.S. (Harvard, Yale, Princeton, Stanford, and MIT) and two in Canada (McGill and the University of Toronto) that almost everyone recognizes as being top-notch colleges. A degree from one of these schools probably *will* impress employers and other people. Furthermore, because the sons and daughters of so many wealthy and influential people attend these institutions, they are good places to make potential career contacts.

Outside of these colleges, however, the name or reputation of a school really means very little. In fact, most people are far more familiar with football schools such as Ohio State than they are with top-notch liberal arts colleges such as Amherst or Williams. With the exception of the seven schools listed above, employers and most other folks will normally be completely unimpressed by what college you went to.

As if this weren't enough, the fact is that not all colleges deserve their reputations. Cleveland State University, for example, is a far better school than most people give it credit for. And there is a large and highly respected university in the northeastern United States that in fact may be one of the worst schools on the continent.

Sometimes individual academic departments (history, philosophy, physics, etc.) within a college will have their own reputations. These are no more reliable than the reputations of entire institutions, however.

Solution: Forget prestige and reputation. Make your own best decisions based on your personal research and campus visits. You want a school you can feel comfortable at, not one that you hate but that may (or, more likely, may not) impress people.

You will not automatically be granted admission to the college your mother or father attended.

Most colleges view applications from the sons and daughters of alumni slightly more favorably than they do other applications. The key word here, however, is *slightly*. In a borderline case, having an alumnus or alumna for a parent will often tip the scales in your favor.

But if you would clearly be denied admission otherwise, being the son or daughter of a graduate isn't likely to make a difference.

At *some* colleges, a large past or present donation to the school from your parents may also be a point in your favor. But, again, if your application would normally receive a clear "no," it's probably still going to get a "no" unless the donation is truly enormous—and even then you may still be turned down.

Solution: Don't try to rest on your parents' laurels—or on their checkbook. At every school to which you apply, submit the very best application you can.

Advice or information about a college from its alumni can be highly inaccurate unless they are recent graduates. Even then much of what they say may be unreliable.

Some colleges—Oberlin or Auburn, for example—seem to stay pretty much the same from year to year. But many go through considerable changes as new administrators come and go, as new programs are added and old ones dropped, and as our world and society evolve. What may have been the case at Hypothetical University in 1989 may no longer be the case at all.

Furthermore, any information you get from an alumnus or alumna will have been processed through that person's own eyes and brain. What he or she tells you may thus be biased, or at least less than objective.

Solution: Listen to what alumni have to say with interest. However, take what they say with a small dose of salt. If they have been away from campus for more than a year or two, use a significantly larger dose.

Sounding scholarly in college admissions essays can work against you.

Some of your high school teachers, and perhaps even your high school guidance counselor, may think that college admissions officers want you to write in a stiff, pompous style. They're wrong; in fact, the exact opposite is true. (Some of these same teachers may expect you to write in a stiff, pompous style for their classes, but they're just as wrong about this; see page 103 for details.)

Good writing is clear, straightforward, and easy to read and follow.

If you don't believe me, ask any college writing teacher, or consult any college-level writing text. For that matter, consult your own common sense.

Admissions people don't want to read high-handed, tight-assed language. They want to see good, clear writing, and they want you to write in your own natural style. In short, they want to get to know more about who you are through your writing. (Of course, they also want you to use correct, grammatical English.)

Furthermore, admissions officers can spot inauthentic prose instantly—and they won't appreciate having to read it.

Solution: Be yourself in your admissions essays and in your responses to the questions on college applications. Use your own regular style; don't try to sound like someone else, or like some imaginary scholar.

Do, however, consider each of your responses carefully, and take the time to write, rewrite, edit, and proofread each one. Use correct grammar, punctuation, and spelling, and write as clearly and straightforwardly as you can.

If you are concerned about your ability to write clear, correct English, have someone (perhaps a parent or friend) look over what you've written and critique it. Also feel free to have someone read the final version of each of your essays and responses, and check it for errors in spelling, punctuation, grammar, and typing. (You may not, of course, have someone else write or rewrite any of your responses for you.)

Applying for Early Decision or Early Action admission to more than one college may get you rejected from both schools.

When you apply for Early Decision admission to a college, you are telling that college that it is your irrevocable first-choice school. In exchange for this preferred status, the school agrees to make a quick, early decision on your application. If you are granted admission to that school, you are then expected to enroll in it (though you usually have the option of delaying your admission by a term or a year if you wish).

A few colleges have what they call Early Action admission, which is identical to Early Decision admission except that you are not required to enroll at the college which says yes to your Early Action application. However, you still may not apply for either Early Action or Early Decision at more than one college.

Some colleges—mostly the Ivy League schools and some other very selective colleges—exchange the names of their Early Decision/ Early Action applicants. If your name appears on more than one college's list, both colleges may shout "foul!" and respond by rejecting you.

Solution: Follow the rules. Apply for Early Decision or Early Action admission only if one school is your clear first choice—and, of course, file only one such application. Doing otherwise is potentially dangerous.

Some colleges may neither admit you nor turn you down, but let you hang, sometimes for months, by putting you on a waiting list.

Waiting lists work like this: Suppose that Imaginary College plans to admit five hundred students to its freshman class. It receives two thousand applications for these five hundred places, and it knows from experience that about forty-eight percent of the students it offers admission to will actually enroll. So it accepts the top thousand of its two thousand applicants, and puts, say, the seventy-five best applicants who did not quite qualify for admission on a waiting list. These seventy-five students are informed that *if* space becomes available, they will then be offered admission.

These seventy-five students may be put on the list one at a time, in descending order of qualification, or they may be divided into groups of five to fifteen, with the groups ranked in descending order.

What happens next depends on what the thousand students who were granted admission choose to do. If five hundred or more students accept the college's offer of admission, then nobody on the waiting list will be offered a place in the freshman class. However, if only 480 choose to enroll, then the top forty students on the waiting list will be offered admission; if 450 students enroll, the top eighty or ninety will be offered places in the freshman class. (Since not all of the people from the waiting list who are offered admission will accept it at such a late date, the college will offer admission to more students than it has places for.)

If you are wait-listed at your first-choice college, do you say no to other schools, and hope and pray that eventually you are offered admission? Or do you say yes to your second-choice college, opting for safety and security?

This problem is further complicated by the fact that students who are admitted off a waiting list often receive poorer financial aid packages for their first year than they would have received if they had been directly admitted (see page 38 for details).

Solution 1: Begin by gathering as much information as you can. Call the admissions office of the college(s) that wait-listed you. Ask politely but directly, "How many people are on the waiting list, and where am I on that list?" If the admissions officer won't give you an exact position, ask which quarter of the list you are in (e.g., the top quarter, bottom quarter, etc.). Then ask for his frank estimate of what your chances are of eventually being offered admission.

Whatever he says, *don't* accept admission at any other school just yet. Wait until the day before your second-choice college must have a response. On that day, call the college(s) that wait-listed you again; find out how long the list is now, where you are on it, and what your chances are of getting in. Then make the best decision you can, and notify the other college(s) of that decision by fax.

If financial aid is an important consideration, and you have been offered a good financial aid package at your second-choice school, you are usually better off taking it. Even if you do eventually get admitted to your first-choice college, by that time it may have little financial aid left, and may thus offer you an inferior aid package for the first year.

Solution 2: Just before the deadline date, accept the offer of admission from your second-choice school, and pay the nonrefundable enrollment deposit due at this time. This can run up to about four hundred dollars. If your first-choice school later offers you admission (and, if you applied for financial aid, an aid package you can live with), turn right around and accept admission there as well. Then withdraw from your second-choice school. You will forfeit your enrollment deposit, but otherwise there will be no penalty. This strategy gives you more options than Solution 1 above, but it can be expensive.

Solution 3: Accept admission elsewhere, then reapply to your first-choice school in the following year as a transfer student.

Solution 4: Enroll at your first-choice school as a nondegree student. If you are eventually accepted as a degree candidate, great. If not, do the best work you can, and reapply for admission as a degree candidate the following year.

The major, program, and/or department that most interests you at a college may no longer be there by the time you are a senior—or even by the time you're a freshman.

Colleges respond to the interests of their students. If hundreds and hundreds of students at Theoretical Institute want to major in business, the college will probably expand its business program and hire more business instructors. But if interest in business courses and the business major shrinks, the college will not replace one of its business instructors who quits or retires. It may also choose to eliminate the business major entirely.

Although it is not a common occurrence, entire programs, majors, and departments may come and go in response to student interest. What may be alive and kicking one year may be gone the next—although never without clear and sufficient warning.

Solution: If a particular major, department, or program especially interests you, look it up in the current course schedule (*not* the college catalog). If a wide range of courses and/or sections is listed (say, twelve or more), you can assume that it is doing just fine. If fewer courses or sections are listed, however, call the department secretary or program director. Explain that you're interested in applying to the college, and are thinking of majoring in the department or enrolling in the program. Ask straightforwardly if the major or program will continue for the next few years. Also ask if any changes in the program or major are planned or contemplated.

If, after you declare a major, that major is dropped from the curriculum, don't despair. Your college is required to permit you to complete and graduate with that major. If a major is dropped before you declare it, however, you will have to find a different one—or, if your college will permit it, you can design your own.

2
Financial Aid

The information in this chapter is directed primarily at students who live and attend (or are planning to attend) college in the United States, and who are being financially supported by their parents. If you are financially independent of your parents, replace the words "your parents" with "you" as you read this chapter, and pay special attention to the section that begins on page 48).

Most of this chapter does *not* apply to students attending or planning to attend college outside of the United States. Much of the chapter also does not apply to people who are not U.S. citizens, nationals, or permanent residents.

For detailed information on financial aid, you and/or your parents should consult the following resources:

Lovejoy's Guide to Financial Aid by Anna Leider (Monarch Press, 1991). This is the single best and most thorough overview of college financial aid.

Don't Miss Out: The Ambitious Student's Guide to Financial Aid by Robert and Anna Leider (Octameron Associates, 1990). Also excellent.

Financial Aid Fin-Ancer by Joseph Re (Octameron Associates, 1990). This first-rate guide answers many difficult questions about financial aid.

Putting Your Kids Through College by Scott Edelstein (Consumer Reports Books, 1989). This is a useful and practical guide written specifically for parents.

How to Find Out About Financial Aid by Gail Ann Schlacter (Reference Service Press, 1987; a new edition will be published in 1992). This is a very useful guide to all of the more than seven hundred sources of information on college financial aid.

Some colleges may offer you less financial aid than you genuinely need—even if they can afford more.

Determining the amount of financial aid you qualify for is a complicated process which involves many different considerations: the college's financial aid budget; the school's overall financial health; your academic record, promise, and/or progress; your family's finances; the amount of financial aid being provided from outside sources (your employer, a fund or foundation, the state, the federal government, etc.); federal, state, and college regulations; and, in some cases, how badly the school wants you to enroll.

Financial aid officers must weigh all of these factors, and frequently several others, to decide how much and what kinds of financial aid to offer you. Colleges can therefore differ significantly in the amount of money they will expect you and your parents to pay. Some colleges may simply not be willing or able to offer you the amount of aid you genuinely need.

Solution 1: Although college financial aid offices don't advertise this fact, a financial aid package can sometimes be improved if you and your parents can show that you need or deserve more. If you honestly feel that the financial aid package you have been offered is inadequate, follow these steps:

First, sit down with your parents and go through all the numbers carefully to make sure they are correct. Then decide exactly how much more aid you will need in order to be able to attend.

Next, one of your parents should call the college's financial aid office, ask to speak to an aid officer, and say something like this: "We appreciate your offer of financial aid very much, and my child very much wants to attend your college. But the aid package you've offered us just won't bridge the gap between the total cost and what we can afford. Is there any way the package can be increased or improved?" Your mother or father should make this request politely, and should neither grovel nor make demands.

It may sometimes help if your mother or father suggests a specific alteration in the college's portion of the aid package, such as changing a $1,000 college-based loan to a $1,000 grant, or to a $500 loan and $500 more in work-study. (Do not try to increase the size of any federal or state grant, however. These are set by national and state policy and cannot be changed.)

If a different college has also admitted you, and is asking for a smaller financial contribution from your family, your father or mother might also say, "_____ College has offered us a financial aid package which only requires a $_____ contribution from us. We can manage that amount, and it seems more in keeping with our financial situation. Can you lower our family contribution to that amount?"

Colleges' policies on adjusting aid packages vary. Some schools may see the logic in your parents' argument and give you more aid (though not necessarily as much as you want or need); others will simply say, "We've made our one and only offer; take it or leave it." When a genuine need exists, colleges will come up with more money about half the time.

If a school simply cannot or will not come up with the aid you need, your parents may wish to say again to the financial aid office, "I'm sorry, but unless you can find a way to come up with $_____ more this year, my child will have to go to school elsewhere." *This should not be a threat, but a simple statement of fact* (which means your parents should not say it unless it is one hundred percent true). When faced with such an ultimatum, perhaps one school in four will find a way to come up with more money.

For excellent detailed information on improving an inadequate aid package, see *Lovejoy's Guide to Financial Aid.*

Important: *Never* try to improve an aid package simply to squeeze more money out of a college. You and your parents should ask for more aid only if you genuinely need it in order to be able to attend. Financial aid is designed to make college affordable—but not comfortably affordable.

Solution 2: Consider asking your parents to borrow the difference (up to $4,000 a year) in a PLUS (Parent Loans to Undergraduate Students) loan. If you are independent of your parents, you may borrow up to $4,000 yourself through an SLS (Supplemental Loan to

Students) loan. Virtually every student or parent is eligible for one of these loans; interest on them is fairly high, however—between ten and twelve percent. See *Lovejoy's Guide* for details.

Before taking out a PLUS or SLS loan, discuss with your parents who will repay it, and how and when it will be repaid. Keep in mind that you or your parents will probably need to take out such a loan for each year that you will be in college.

Solution 3: Ask a financial aid officer if the college offers an installment payment program. Many schools now offer this option, either on their own or in conjunction with a financial institution. These programs vary widely; some simply split each term's bills into two or three parts, while others spread the year's expense over nine to twelve monthly payments. Most installment plans require parents to pay a participation fee or interest charge.

If your college does not offer an installment payment program, your parents may wish to consider one of the installment programs offered directly to parents by financial institutions. These programs essentially offer secured or unsecured short-term college loans at reasonable rates of interest. See the list of financial institutions at the end of Solution 4.

Solution 4: Many financial institutions now offer secured and/or unsecured credit lines. Some of these line-of-credit plans are specifically for paying college costs; others are all-purpose plans.

Under such a plan, your parents write checks to pay college expenses (up to the limit of their credit line), then repay whatever they have borrowed, plus interest, over the months or years to come.

The organizations listed below have sponsored installment and/or credit-line payment plans for some time. In recent years, however, a great many other financial institutions have begun offering these options. Your parents may wish to check with local lenders about one of these plans.

Tuition Management Systems
Box 335
Newport, RI 02840
800-722-4867

The Education Credit Corporation
501 Silverside Road, Suite 125
Wilmington, DE 19809
800-999-5626

Collegeaire
Student Financial Services
Box 88370
Atlanta, GA 30356
404-952-2500

Academic Management Services
50 Vision Boulevard
Box 14608
East Providence, RI 02914-0608
800-635-0120

Educational Financing Group
57 Regional Drive
Concord, NH 03301
800-822-8764

Knight Tuition Payment Plan
855 Boylston Street
Boston, MA 02116
800-225-6783

Mellon Bank Delaware
4500 New Linden Road
Wilmington, DE 19808
Attn: June Pittman
302-992-7753

Solution 5: Take out a college loan from a private educational loan program. The following organizations sponsor a variety of loan programs. Some offer loans directly to parents and students; others work through participating banks and credit unions; still others work through individual colleges. One organization, ConSern, also offers loans through employers.

Private loan programs are offered by:

The Education Resource Institute
330 Stuart Street, Suite 500
Boston, MA 02116
800-255-8374

ConSern
205 Van Buren Street, Suite 200
Herndon, VA 22070
800-767-5626

New England Education Loan Marketing
    Corporation
50 Braintree Hill Park, Suite 300
Braintree, MA 02184
800-634-9308

SALLIE MAE
1050 Thomas Jefferson Street NW
Washington, DC 20007
800-831-5626

When an organization does not offer loans directly, ask for the names of participating lenders in your area.

These loans carry a higher rate of interest than PLUS and SLS loans. In general, I recommend first taking out a PLUS or SLS loan, and taking out a loan from a private lender only if the PLUS or SLS loan isn't enough.

Your parents can also, of course, look into college loans and home equity loans from any other financial institution of their choice.

Solution 6: The best way to avoid this problem is to provide each college's financial aid office with complete and detailed financial information in the first place.

Thoroughly, carefully, and honestly fill out any required standardized aid forms (the FAF, the FFS, the SingleFile, etc.) and each college's own financial aid form. In addition, you and your parents should give each financial aid office a list of unusual expenses that the family expects to incur in the following year: costs for medical treatments, operations, orthodontia, prescription medications, a new hearing aid, etc.; necessary home improvement costs (such as the cost of replacing an old, damaged roof); the cost of a computer, peripherals, and software for your use in college (an especially significant expense at colleges that expect or require all students to own computers); and any other anticipated nonstandard costs. The more upcoming costs a college is aware of, the more financial aid you are likely to receive (and the more likely you are to receive financial aid in the first place).

Solution 7: Apply to at least one college that your family can definitely afford to pay for without any financial aid at all, or with a PLUS loan of $4,000 or less per year. This should of course be a school you genuinely want to attend.

If, after you have accepted admission and a financial aid package from a college, you and/or your parents are unable to pay your share of the required family contribution, you may not be permitted to enroll at that school.

Suppose, for example, that Costly College's financial aid office sets your family contribution at $9,000 ($7,500 from your parents and $1,500 from your savings and summer income). Since Costly runs on the quarter system, the family contribution for the academic year works out to $1,875 per quarter for your parents and $375 per quarter for you. During the summer, however, your parents realize that they simply cannot come up with enough money to pay the first quarter's bill for tuition and fees. But if these charges are not paid in full, your registration will be canceled, and you'll suddenly be a nonstudent.

Solution: If a financial crisis appears imminent, your parents should call the college's financial aid office immediately to candidly explain and discuss the problem. Special arrangements can often (though not always) be made.

Getting in touch with the financial aid office is particularly important if your family has a large, unexpected financial loss or expense. Some financial aid offices may be willing to improve your aid package under these circumstances.

Financial aid offices are especially willing to be flexible in the event of a separation or divorce, the loss of a full-time job, the death of a parent, or the loss of alimony, child support, unemployment benefits, AFDC, etc. In fact, under these circumstances, the federal government may be willing to recalculate your eligibility for a Pell Grant, or the size of that grant.

Solutions 2, 3, 4, and 5 in the section above may also prove helpful.

Different colleges may disagree greatly about the amount of your family's financial need.

In part, this is as it should be. An expensive college *should* give you more financial aid than an inexpensive one, simply because the gap between what you can afford and what the school costs is greater.

Imagine, for example, that you apply to both Cut-Rate State College (which charge $5,800 per year for tuition, fees, room, and board) and Upscale University (which charges $18,000). Both schools admit you, and both offer you financial aid. But Cut-Rate assesses your family's financial need at only $2,000 per year, while Upscale says that you deserve a whopping $14,200 in assistance. Which school is correct?

They both are. Both colleges determined that, together, you and your parents will be able to contribute $3,800 toward one year of college. This amount that you are determined to be able to pay is known in financial aid jargon as your *family contribution.* Your financial need at each college is determined by deducting the amount of your family contribution from the total cost of tuition, fees, housing, and meals, plus the estimated cost of books, supplies, transportation, and necessary personal expenses. Thus your financial need can vary widely from school to school.

What should *not* vary widely is the amount of your required family contribution. Unfortunately, however, this does sometimes differ significantly from school to school. When it does, it means that the college asking for a larger family contribution either feels it needs the money or is simply more tightfisted than the school that asks for less.

Solution: Don't worry about any college's "sticker price"—the total cost of all the items listed above. What should most concern you and your parents is the amount of the family contribution that each college expects.

If two or more colleges do disagree on how much money your family should contribute, your parents may be able to use the smaller family contribution required by one college to convince the other school to lower the amount of money it expects from your family. See page 24 for details.

Not all schools make admissions and financial aid decisions separately. And even if a college does make separate admissions and financial aid decisions, the size and makeup of your financial aid package may still be based in part on how much the college wants you.

As I explained on page 11, some private colleges (but not state or community colleges) will take your family's finances into account when deciding whether or not to admit you. At some of these schools, poverty can get you rejected just as easily as poor grades. (More likely, though, you'll be accepted but offered a financial aid package that doesn't begin to meet your needs—and you'll have to say no to the school, instead of the other way around.)

Admission and financial aid decisions can become joined in another way: A school that really wants you may be more generous with aid (and require a lower family contribution) than one that is less enthusiastic about you. Even colleges that make separate admissions and financial aid decisions sometimes do this.

Solution: Follow the advice in the first section of this chapter on improving an adequate financial aid package.

Colleges will not take into account all your necessary expenses unless you provide them with a list of those expenses. Most financial aid forms do not ask for such a list.

If you have—or will have—any unusual expenses, it is up to you to let college financial aid offices know about them. The more expenses a financial aid office is aware of, the lower your family contribution is likely to be.

Solution: Before you and your parents fill out any financial aid applications, sit down together and make a complete and careful list of all your family's anticipated expenses for the upcoming academic year. Pay special attention to any unusual or onetime expenses, such as the cost of moving, or corrective surgery, or a new car to replace your family's worn-out jalopy. Also include eyeglasses, required prescription medications, insurance and/or HMO membership, child care, costs related to a disability, etc. If you anticipate high transportation expenses, list these as well.

Your parents should write up a complete list of all of these expenses, including the estimated costs of each and the total cost of all of them for the academic year, and attach this list to each college's financial aid application. They should *not* attach it to any standardized national or state financial aid application such as the FAF, the FFS, or the SingleFile.

If you do not fill in certain financial aid forms completely, they may not be processed. And if you do not use the specific form a college or state requires, you may be denied all need-based aid.

If you wish to receive need-based financial aid, you'll have to fill out at least one "need analysis form": a fill-in-the-blank form which will be read by a computer. There are three major such forms: the FAF (Financial Aid Form), the FFS (Family Financial Statement), and the SingleFile form. Two states, Illinois and Pennsylvania, require their own forms, the Application for Federal and State Student Aid (Illinois) and the Application for Pennsylvania State Grant and Federal Student Aid (Pennsylvania). Certain states also require special state versions of the FAF or FFS (there is no special state version of the SingleFile).

Each college makes its own decision about which one of these forms to require, though some schools will allow you to choose from among two or more different options. Many state financial aid programs also require you to file a specific form. In practice, many students only have to file one need analysis form, but many others are required to file two or even three.

Since these forms are read by computers, and since computers are notoriously inflexible, it is imperative that you fill out each of these forms completely and accurately. If you skip even one answer or forget to fill in a single blank, your loan application may not be processed. And if you do not file the specific form a state or college requires, it will simply refuse to process your aid application at all.

Solution: Do as you're told. File whatever forms you have to, and do so as close to January 1 as possible—but not before (forms postmarked before January 1 will not be processed).

If a college or state aid program permits you to choose between two or more different forms but states a preference for a particular one, definitely file this form, even if it means "needless extra work." Using the preferred form may give you a slight advantage in receiving aid.

Your eligibility for financial aid, and the amount of aid you receive, may be based on out-of-date financial information.

Financial aid offices base their aid awards largely on your and your parents' tax returns for previous calendar year. For example, your aid award for the 1992-93 academic year (which will be announced in the spring of 1992) will be based heavily on your family's 1991 tax returns. If your and your parents' 1991 returns don't adequately reflect your current financial situation, you could end up with significantly less aid than you genuinely need.

Solution: Don't let this happen. The moment there is any significant change in your or your family's income or expenses, let college financial aid offices know. Be prepared to provide written evidence of these changes.

Financial aid offices are not charities, but they **can** be flexible; if you can show that you need more aid because your financial circumstances have changed, most will do their best to improve your aid package.

Providing college financial aid offices with a complete list of your and your family's anticipated expenses, as described on pages 30–31, can also help enormously. The more hard information financial aid people have, the more they will be willing and able to do on your behalf.

In order to receive certain forms of federal financial aid, you will need to make several promises: that you won't use illegal drugs, that you aren't in default on a student loan, that you don't owe the federal

government a refund from an earlier education grant, that you will only use federal funds for educational purposes (room and board count as educational purposes so long as you remain a student), and, if you're a male and old enough, that you have registered for the draft.

Recent regulations require students to sign several pledges and promises in order to receive federal money. The drug-free pledge is required in order to receive a Pell Grant, but not for other forms of federal financial aid. The other promises are required for you to receive **any** form of federal financial aid, including an SLS loan, or even a PLUS loan. *Unless you sign off on all of the above items, neither of your parents can borrow a PLUS loan.*

Some individual colleges have their own statements to sign as well. These typically reiterate some or all of the items listed above.

Solution: Sign whatever you have to. If you're a male, register for the draft as soon as you turn eighteen. If you owe the federal government or a lender money on a previous loan or from an earlier grant, you will have to make some payback arrangements before you can receive further aid.

As for the drug-free pledge, this is a touchy issue. When you sign, you promise not to "make, distribute, dispense, possess, or use" any illegal drug during the entire period covered by your Pell Grant. You also promise to notify the U.S. Department of Education if you are convicted of a drug-related offense committed during that period.

What does all this mean? It does **not** mean that the federal government will send out spies after you, that it suspects you of drug use already, or that if you are found guilty of using illegal drugs you will also be tried for fraud. It **does** mean that if you don't sign the drug-free pledge, you won't get a Pell Grant. It also means that if you are found guilty of illegal drug use and are receiving federal educational aid of **any** type, you may have part or all of that aid cut off.

In practice, then, you should either not use illegal drugs at all—or, if you do choose to use them, use them very discreetly and privately.

Colleges will almost always drastically underestimate the amount you will have to spend on personal expenses during the academic year. Often they will underestimate the cost of books and transportation as well.

Each college makes its own estimate of what its students will have to pay for personal expenses, transportation, and books during the academic year. It then uses these estimates in determining financial aid and family contributions for all of its students who receive need-based aid.

However, these estimates vary significantly from school to school. Estimates for personal expenses range from under $800 to over $1,300; for transportation, from under $200 to close to $1,000; and for books, from under $400 to over $700.

Some schools' estimated costs for books and/or transportation are fairly close to the mark; others' estimates are far too low. Virtually every college, however, drastically underestimates students' personal expenses.

"Personal expenses" refers to all costs except for room, board, tuition, fees, books, educational supplies, and transportation. This category thus includes all clothing, insurance, car expenses, medical and dental expenses, dates, laundry, luxuries, emergencies, and much, much more.

Solution: Don't take colleges' estimates seriously when determining your actual expenses and planning a budget for the school year. Instead, make your own list of all the expenses you are likely to incur. Be thorough, and include the realistic cost over the academic year for each item; for safety's sake, overestimate each cost by about ten percent. Use *these* figures to plan your budget.

The costs of transportation and books can vary greatly from student to student. It's difficult to estimate these in advance. Keep a record of your actual expenses during your first term; the cost in future terms will likely be roughly the same, or slightly higher.

If your parents wish, they may use these actual costs to push for more generous aid packages from financial aid offices.

Colleges will expect you to give them most of your savings and other assets—but they will want a far smaller percentage of your parents'.

Your family's contribution to college costs consists of two parts: the amount the financial aid office expects your parents to pay, and the amount it expects *you* to pay.

Colleges know that your parents have a family to support, mortgage and car payments to make, and innumerable other expenses to take care of. They also know (or at least assume) that you have few or no such commitments. Therefore, when calculating your family contribution, financial aid offices will normally ask for only a small percentage of your parents' income and assets. However, they will insist on a much higher percentage—about six times higher—of *your* assets and income.

Solution: Just before you begin applying to colleges, arrange with your parents to have most or all of your savings and other assets (savings bonds, stocks, etc.) put in one or both of your parents' names. This strategy alone could significantly reduce your college costs and increase your financial aid. If you wish, make an agreement with your parents to have what remains of these assets placed back in your name when you graduate.

Some parents, on the advice of financial planners, do just the opposite: They place some of their assets in their child's name, so that the growth on those assets will be taxed at a lower rate. However, for financial aid purposes, this can be disastrous; indeed, it could end up reducing your financial aid to zero. Unless your family is so well off that you are unlikely to qualify for need-based financial aid in the first place, the financial aid benefits of putting your assets in your parents' names far outweigh the tax savings that might be generated if your parents placed some of their assets in your name.

Show this section to your parents. For more details on the subject, have them consult *Lovejoy's Guide* and/or *Putting Your Kids Through College*.

A scholarship isn't necessarily free money. Many scholarships are loans that must be repaid.

Actually, the word "scholarship" can refer to almost any type of financial aid: a grant, a loan, a tuition discount, or even a job or a payment program. Receiving a scholarship means you're entitled to some money; but you may have to work for that money or eventually pay it back.

Solution: Don't get too excited when you find out you've gotten a scholarship. First find out exactly what the terms of the scholarship are. You might have received a grant—or you might have gotten something far less valuable.

If you win a merit scholarship from your college, this won't necessarily improve your financial aid package or decrease the amount you and your parents will have to pay toward college costs. And if you come up with an outside grant, loan, or other form of financial aid on your own, this may not reduce your family contribution, either.

Financial aid accounting can be tricky. Let's say that your college determines that your family's financial need is $7,000, and it provides an aid package of $2,700 in grants, $1,300 in work-study, and $3,000 in loans. Your family contribution is set at $8,900.

A few weeks later, however, the physics department awards you its prestigious Neutron Scholarship, worth $2,000. Does this lower your family contribution to $6,900?

Perhaps—but perhaps not. Your college might simply apply your scholarship against your financial need and reduce your grant money from $2,700 to $700, leaving you with a net gain of zero. If it was more generous, it might apply part or all of the scholarship against your loans, so that although your family contribution doesn't shrink, at least you don't have to borrow as much. In any case, the college may not ask less than $8,900 from your family.

The situation is the same with financial assistance that you have arranged on your own through an outside source. If you receive a grant from your church, or your employer, or a foundation, it is up to your college's financial aid office to decide what to do with it. You might get some or all of it in cash (highly unlikely unless it exceeds the amount of your financial need); or, some or all of it might be used to reduce your loans or work-study commitment; or, it all might disappear into your college's coffers with no effect on you or your family whatsoever.

Solution: Don't ask or expect your college to use unexpected or outside money to reduce your family contribution.

However, don't expect to have nothing at all to show for this windfall, either. It is rather sleazy for a school to take the money without adjusting the makeup of your aid package. You should expect your college to use at least half (if not all) of these funds to offset loans and/or work-study.

If your college doesn't do this, your parents may wish to discuss the matter with a financial aid officer. They should express their dismay at the school's decision and specifically ask that the money be used to reduce the size of your loans and/or work-study grant. There is a reasonable chance that this request will be granted.

If a college awards you a $1,000 work-study grant, it is *not* obligated to provide you with $1,000 worth of work.

Work-study grants are a bit odd. First of all, they're not grants, and they involve no studying. They are simply college-sponsored jobs provided to students. They are invariably part-time (usually six to fifteen hours per week), and they usually pay little or no more than the minimum wage.

Let's say your college gives you a $1,000 work-study grant. This doesn't mean that your school guarantees you $1,000 worth of employment during the school year. All it means is that it will give you this much employment if it can. Nor is the $1,000 figure an upper limit: The college has the right to offer you additional work at your regular salary if it wishes. (You are not obligated to accept this additional work.)

Solution: In practice, colleges will almost always find you at least seventy-five percent of the work they promise you—and most students end up with one hundred percent of what they are promised.

But since most work-study jobs pay such meager salaries, you may be better off (perhaps far better off) finding an off-campus job, or creating your own.

The fact is you don't have to accept *any* work-study job, even if it is part of your financial aid package. Turning down a work-study job will not affect the rest of your aid package, and it won't hurt your chances of getting other forms of financial aid in the future. However, you will still have to come up with the amount of money you would have earned had you accepted the work-study grant.

Some financial aid offices will allow you to replace some or all of a work-study grant with a loan from the college. More often, however, students simply find jobs that pay as well or better on their own, and use the money they earn from these jobs to pay college costs. Others start their own entreprenurial ventures: Some type or edit others' papers; some sell sandwiches in the college quad; some make and sell items of clothing; and some come up with their own new and successful business schemes.

Some financial aid is given on a first-come, first-served basis. Late applicants for aid, and students admitted from waiting lists, may therefore receive reduced or inferior financial aid packages.

The reason for this is simple: By the time these students are admitted, nearly all of the college's financial aid budget for the year may already be spoken for.

Solution 1: Have your parents speak with a financial aid administrator. Perhaps they can get your aid package improved, at least a little, by following the guidelines on pages 23–24.

You and your parents will also need to get some reassurance from the financial aid office that next year you will be given a much fairer shake at financial assistance. If you can get such an assurance—and probably you can—then it may well be worth biting the bullet and incurring some extra debt during your first year, in the expectation that things will be better thereafter.

If you cannot get this assurance, however, then your financial aid package next year could be just as dismal as this year's. Seriously consider enrolling in a different college, one that is more sensitive to your family's financial circumstances and needs.

Solution 2: Accept the college's offer of admission, but defer your enrollment for one year, and reapply for financial aid during the following year's application cycle. Most colleges will permit you to do this; check with the admissions and financial aid offices for details.

The big plus of this strategy is that it puts you back into the running for your full share of financial aid. The drawback, of course, is that you cannot attend the college of your choice for another year. However, during this year you can work, study on your own, and/or take some courses at another school as a nondegree student. You can then transfer in these courses when you enroll the following year. See page 79 for guidelines on this topic.

Your college may require you to pay college charges *before* you receive certain forms of financial aid.

If you receive a $1,500 work-study grant, this doesn't mean that you get a check (or even a credit against your tuition bill) for $1,500 at the beginning of the school year. All it means is that the college will give you a job and pay you regular wages. Fifteen hundred dollars in work-study actually means fifteen twice-monthly paychecks of $100 each (in fact, less after taxes).

Nevertheless, if your college has two terms during the academic year, you will be expected to pay $750 at the beginning of the first term and $750 at the beginning of the second—*in addition to your part of the family contribution*. In essence, then, you must come up with this money before you have earned it. And because taxes are taken from your earnings, you must pay the college more than you earn.

This isn't the only situation in which bills may come due before you receive the financial aid to pay them. Federal grant money (and, in some cases, state grant money as well) typically does not arrive until the second or third week of the term. Sometimes grants and loans may be delayed longer because of bureaucratic foul-ups. You may thus find yourself still waiting for your aid when the deadline to pay your bill arrives.

Solution 1: Plan ahead. If you receive a $1,500 work-study grant, be aware that this means you'll have to come up with $750 at or before the beginning of each semester (or $375 at or before the beginning of each quarter). In practice, this means earning this sum during the summer, along with whatever additional amount you are expected to pay as your part of the first term family contribution. What you earn during your first term will then go to pay your second-term bill, and so on. Another option: Earn the full amount of your work-study contribution during the summer, and use your meager earnings from your work-study job as pocket money.

Solution 2: As for bills that come due before financial aid arrives, don't panic. One week before the bill is due, call or visit your school's financial aid office. Explain the situation in detail and promise to pay the bill on the day the money arrives.

But don't stop there. Ask the financial aid representative to do two things for you: First, waive any late fees, and second, make sure that your registration does not get canceled. It is extremely important that they take care of both of these items for you, because at most schools computers automatically kick in late fees or kick out students if they have not paid their bills by a certain date.

Be sure to get the full name of the person you talk to, so that if there is any problem later, you can go back to him directly to have him square things for you.

I know of no college where the financial aid people will not be willing to accommodate you under these circumstances—even if the reason for the delay in receiving your aid is your own tardiness in filing the appropriate forms.

Plan your expenses accordingly as well. If you know a financial aid check won't show up until the second week of the term, set enough money aside in advance to buy your books for the term and get through the first two or three weeks.

Some financial aid—work-study, assistantships, certain scholarships, and any aid that covers room, board, transportation, and/or personal expenses—is one hundred percent taxable by the IRS.

Whenever you are paid a salary in exchange for performing a service—whether that service is tutoring other students, assisting an instructor in her research, washing pots in a college dining hall, or shelving books in the library—all money you earn from that endeavor is subject to federal and state (and sometimes local) income taxes. There's one common exception, however: If part or all of your tuition and/or fees are waived in exchange for your services, the amount of the waiver is not taxable. (Waivers of room or board charges *are* subject to federal, and usually state, income taxes, though.)

Certain grants are taxable as well. Grants used to pay for tuition, fees, books, and educational supplies are not subject to federal tax. But grant money used for *any* other expenses is considered taxable income by the IRS. This holds true even if you never actually see any of the grant money.

For example, suppose your college charges $2,100 in tuition and fees and $3,900 for room and board for one academic year. The college awards you a scholarship grant of $4,500, half of which it deducts from your total bill each semester. You never actually see a check—just a bill for $750 a few weeks before the beginning of each semester. However, $2,400 of your grant—the portion which covers housing and meals—is considered income, and is subject to tax.

Solution: Take all of this carefully into account when planning your budget for the academic year. Remember that a dollar in earnings from a work-study job or assistantship will leave you with only about eighty cents in spending power. And keep in mind that some of the "free" money you receive may actually cost you up to several hundred dollars a year in income taxes. Plan accordingly.

If you must pay $100 or more in income tax on your financial aid money in your first year of college, include this amount in your list of anticipated expenses for the following academic year. Attach a copy of this list to your college's financial aid application; follow the guidelines on pages 30–31.

Naturally, any taxable financial aid should be listed on your own income tax return, not your parents'—even if they are the ones paying most or all of the family contribution.

You and your parents will need to prepare your federal income taxes in early January in order to provide accurate information on financial aid forms.

It is at least as important to apply early for financial aid as it is to apply early for admission. The earlier you apply, the more of a college's financial aid budget remains uncommitted to other students.

Timing for financial aid applications can be tricky, however. *You and your parents must wait until January 1 to file any standardized financial aid form* (the FFS, the FAF, the SingleFile, etc.) for the upcoming academic year; forms postmarked before then will not be processed. However, it is important to file these forms—as well as colleges' own financial aid forms and your supplementary lists of expenses—absolutely as soon thereafter as possible. Plan to send in all of these items during the first two weeks of January—at the very latest, by the twenty-fifth of the month.

In order to file these forms, you and your parents will both need to have prepared (though not necessarily filed) your income taxes for the previous year. It thus becomes very important that all of you prepare your income taxes as early as possible.

Solution: Talk to your parents about income taxes in November or early December. Explain the importance of preparing their taxes in early January and filing financial aid forms as soon as possible thereafter. Show them this section of this book as well.

Do your own taxes during the first week in January. Do not wait for W-2s before preparing your returns; if you or your parents need any information from one of your W-2s, call your employer(s) and get it over the phone.

In mid-December, you and your parents should contact your employers and ask that your W-2s be sent out as early as possible. If any W-2 hasn't arrived by January 15, call and ask that it be sent immediately. If it still hasn't arrived by January 25, call again—but on this same day, submit all your financial aid forms.

Normally you and your parents will be expected to include copies of your complete federal income tax returns with each college financial aid application; under these circumstances, however, send everything you can and attach a note saying that you will forward a copy of the missing W-2 as soon as it arrives.

If you and/or your parents simply cannot complete your taxes by January 25, call each college's financial aid office. Ask if the school will accept estimated figures temporarily, with photocopies of completed tax returns to follow as soon as possible. Most colleges will agree to this, although at some schools this may be a point against you.

If you apply for Early Decision or Early Action admission (see page 18 for details), you and your parents may also be required to submit a standardized form called an Early Version Financial Aid Form, and/or a form designed by the college, before January 1.

The U.S. Department of Education usually publishes its financial aid guide and its standardized application form later than many schools' deadlines for financial aid applications.

The Department of Education puts out an annual guide to its biggest financial aid programs—Pell Grants, Supplemental Educational Opportunity Grants, Stafford Loans, Perkins Loans, PLUS and SLS loans, and the College Work-Study Program. This booklet is entitled *The Student Guide*, and it is usually published in February or late January—but many colleges require financial aid applications to be filed by January 31.

The Department of Education also publishes the Application for

Federal Student Aid (AFSA), its own standardized aid form, at about the same time.

Solution: Forget the AFSA completely. It is totally useless, and there is no reason for anyone to bother with it. I have no idea why the Department of Education bothers to publish it.

Also forget *The Student Guide*, at least temporarily. If you and your parents will outfit yourselves with *Lovejoy's Guide, Putting Your Kids Through College,* and *Financial Aid Fin-Ancer*, you'll have all the tools and information you need to deal with the Department of Education's aid programs. If you have any questions, call the appropriate college's financial aid office.

When February rolls around, it is a good idea to get and read *The Student Guide*, simply to stay as informed as possible and updated on any changes in procedures or policies. Copies are available free at most high school guidance offices and college financial aid offices; you can also order a copy by calling 800-433-3243, or by writing the Federal Student Aid Information Center, Box 84, Washington, DC 20044.

Your financial aid application may be audited, just like an income tax return.

At each college to which you apply for aid, an aid officer will review your entire application carefully. If anything seems odd, contradictory, or amiss, they will get in touch with you or your parents and ask for verification or documentation.

Each year, a small percentage of standardized financial aid applications (the FAF, the FFS, etc.) are also selected at random by the Department of Education to be audited. The Department of Education may also choose to carefully examine any application which seems suspicious or inconsistent—and it, too, may request written verification or documentation of claims that seem odd or unusual. Some state financial aid agencies also do their own verification.

If you or your parents are asked to verify some information, the processing of your aid application will be delayed until the necessary information is received.

Solution: It is essential that you and your parents be scrupulously honest, complete, and forthright about your finances. If any of you are caught trying to lie, mislead, or hide or undervalue assets, you may be denied any and all financial aid for the year.

Your parents *may*, however, list an asset's lowest honest value. For example, if your house has been appraised at both $112,000 and $116,000, it's considered kosher to list the lower appraisal.

If you or your parents are asked to provide verification or documentation of any kind, provide it promptly. If there are any problems, discuss them openly with someone from the appropriate office or agency.

Neither you nor your parents will be penalized for honest mistakes. The verification process often turns up quite a few of these.

Applications for Stafford Loans, PLUS loans, and SLS loans can take months to process.

These loans can take as long as two to three months, and sometimes longer, from the time you file your loan application until the check is actually issued.

Part of the reason for this is that each loan application normally passes through the hands of a state guaranteeing agency, which promises the lender that it will repay your loan if you do not. (This won't let you off the hook, however; guaranteeing agencies are ruthless in pursuing loan defaulters.) These state agencies can take weeks to complete their part of the loan processing.

Solution 1: File your loan application as soon as possible. In the case of Stafford Loans, this means as soon as you have accepted a financial aid package for the following year. For PLUS and SLS loans, this means as soon as you have accepted admission from a college, or fifteen weeks before your first term begins, whichever comes first.

Solution 2: If for some reason you must apply for one of these loans less than three months before classes begin, you can cut two to five weeks off the processing time by using an organization called United Student Aid Funds. This is a private, nonprofit guaranteeing agency which offers one major advantage over state agencies: speed. USA Funds processes loan applications in two to three days instead of two to five weeks.

If you need to cut even more time off your loan processing, use USA Funds' electronic processing service, which reduces the agency's processing time to less than twenty-four hours. There is an extra charge for this service, however, and electronic processing will not speed up other parts of the loan approval process. Also, this option is available only with certain lenders and colleges. (If it isn't available in your case, simply send in your application via Express Mail.)

There are two small catches to using USA funds. First, you or your parents must use a USA Funds loan application form, available free by mail from USA Funds (see address and phone number below), and from some lenders, college financial aid offices, and high school guidance offices.

Second, all guaranteeing agencies charge a guarantee fee. State guaranteeing agencies charge one-half to three percent of the loan, depending on the state. USA Funds, however, charges three percent. Using USA Funds instead of a state guaranteeing agency could thus cost you up to about $100, depending on the size of your loan.

For more information on USA Funds, or to request a USA Funds loan application, write United Student Aid Funds, 11100 USA Parkway, Fishers, IN 46038, or call 800-562-6872.

Computerized scholarship search services are never absolutely comprehensive, no matter what those services may claim.

For $35–$150, you can have a computer prepare a list of many of the forms of financial aid for which you may be eligible. This list can be useful, at least in informing you of some aid sources worth researching further.

The service works like this: You fill out a data sheet with information on yourself, your interests, your background, your academic record, and your and your parents' finances. The computer then checks its data base to see what financial aid programs your age, sex, race, nationality, religion, home state, interests, academic achievement, intended major, and/or financial situation may qualify you for.

Most of these data bases are quite extensive, and they are usually updated four to twelve times a year. However, none is one hundred percent complete. They do not always carry complete and updated information on aid programs sponsored by all fifty states, the District of Columbia, and U.S. possessions. They include only a small percentage of scholarship programs offered by employers. And they simply cannot keep on top of all the changes in existing programs and all the new programs that spring up.

Scholarship search services can therefore be somewhat useful. They can let you know of aid sources that you might otherwise have overlooked (or never heard of). However, a scholarship search is no substitute for your own research.

Solution: In addition to (or instead of) any such computer search, consult one or more of these excellent reference books:

Need a Lift? edited by Terry L. Woodburn (1991; available for $2 postpaid from The American Legion, National Emblem Sales, Box 1050, Indianapolis, IN 46206)

The Scholarship Book by Daniel J. Cassidy and Michael J. Alves (Prentice Hall, 1990)

Chronicle Student Aid Manual (Chronicle Guidance Publications, 1991)

Financial Aids for Higher Education by Oreon Keeslar (William C. Brown, 1991)

Scholarships, Fellowships, and Loans (Gale Research, 1991)

Reference Service Press publishes the following specialized financial aid guides, all edited by Gail Ann Schlachter:

Directory of Financial Aids for Minorities (1991)

Directory of Financial Aids for Women (1991)

Financial Aid for Veterans, Military Personnel, and Their Dependents (with R. David Weber, 1990)

Financial Aid for the Disabled and Their Families (with R. David Weber, 1990)

It's important to understand that the best a scholarship search service can do is inform you of those aid programs to which you are eligible *to apply.* It cannot guarantee you aid from any source.

Some scholarship search services advertise themselves by guaranteeing to find you at least five or six aid programs for which you are eligible. These will be programs for which you are eligible *to apply,* not ones which are certain to offer you money. (This may simply turn out to be the U.S. Department of Education's six major forms of college financial aid.)

Many of the people at the U.S. Department of Education's financial aid telephone information center do not understand the

department's own rules and policies, and will give you advice and answers that are misleading, incomplete, or downright false.

These people are trained to answer only the simplest and most common questions about the Department of Education's aid programs. If you ask them anything out of the ordinary, they will either not know or give you an incorrect answer.

Solution: Don't deal with these people unless you absolutely have to. If you have a question about financial aid, including any question about a Department of Education aid program, call a college financial aid office. (Do not ask a high school guidance counselor, unless the question is a very simple one. Guidance counselors may be no more reliable than Department of Education staff people.) Also consult the helpful books listed on page 22.

If your parents are divorced or separated, one of them may be required to bear the full financial responsibility of putting you through college, while the other may be let entirely off the hook.

The rules for applying for financial assistance can be especially complicated and confusing if your parents are separated or divorced. For one thing, the Department of Education's rules will require that one and only one of your parents file standardized financial aid forms such as the FAF, the FFS, and the SingleFile. (This will normally be the parent you lived with during most of the past year.) That parent then becomes fully and solely responsible for the parental portion of any family contribution—at least as far as the Department of Education is concerned.

Individual colleges, however, have the right to set rules of their own. Some may ask both of your parents to fill out certain financial aid forms, and some may ask for (or insist on) financial contributions from both of them.

Solution: Ask both of your parents to get and read these three books: *Putting Your Kids Through College*, which includes a detailed discussion of financial aid for divorced and separated families; *Financial Aid Fin-Ancer,* which answers many thorny questions on the subject; and *Lovejoy's Guide to Financial Aid*, which provides an excellent overview of the whole financial aid process.

Either or both of your parents should also feel free to speak with college financial aid officers to discuss their situation and/or ask questions.

Even if you are financially independent of your parents, they may still be required to fill out certain financial aid forms, and the amount of financial aid you receive may nevertheless be based on their income as well as yours. This could remain true even if your parents will not contribute a penny toward your education.

The U.S. Department of Education and most states have very specific definitions of who qualifies as a financially independent student and who does not. Ninety-five percent of the time, these definitions make sense. However, it is very possible to be completely financially independent from your parents and still fit the Department of Education's official definition of a dependent; it is also possible to be financially dependent on your parents but be considered officially independent. As you fill out standardized financial aid forms, it will quickly become clear what your official status is.

Solution: Fill out all financial aid forms precisely as you are instructed to—even if the instructions seem inappropriate or absurd. Also have your parents fill out any sections that they are instructed to complete. *If you and your parents don't do exactly what the forms require you to do, your aid application will probably not be processed.*

If you are financially independent of your parents, but do not qualify for independent status according to the Department of Education's definition, explain your situation to a financial aid officer at each college to which you apply. If your parents have refused to fill out their part of any application, mention this as well, and ask for guidance.

Also, when you submit each college's financial aid application, attach to it a letter explaining your circumstances in detail. Do *not* attach such an explanation to any standardized financial aid form such as the FAF, the FFS, or the SingleFile.

Each college's financial aid officer has the power to change your official status from dependent to independent if circumstances warrant it. The more information a financial aid office has, the better job it can do of making such an evaluation.

Moving to another state (or the District of Columbia, or a U.S. possession) to attend college will not normally qualify you for financial aid provided by that state, or for in-state tuition at a public college in that state. This is usually true for at least the first year, and possibly longer, *even if* you become a resident of that state.

Residency for tuition and financial aid purposes is not determined in the same way as residency for voting. Most states have very strict regulations prohibiting residents of other states from paying in-state tuition or receiving financial aid from the state.

These regulations differ widely from state to state. Generally, though, if you move to another state for the purpose of attending college, you are ineligible for in-state tuition or financial aid from that state for your entire college career.

If your *parents* move to that state, though, then you probably *will* become eligible for both state financial aid and in-state tuition. However, there may be a waiting period before you qualify.

Exceptions to all this abound. Depending on the state, you *may* be eligible for in-state tuition and/or in-state financial aid at a school there if:

• You are financially independent of your parents, either in fact or under the Department of Education's official definition.

• You attend school part-time.

• You declare the new state as your state of permanent residence, and can provide evidence that you intend to remain there. (This is usually difficult to do if your parents live outside of the state.)

• You have lived in that state for at least one year.

• You have lived in that state for one year or more without attending college there.

Another wrinkle: A few states offer financial aid to their residents who attend school in another state.

While many states set statewide regulations on residency and financial aid, in other states the regulations vary from school to school. What may be the case at one public college may therefore not be the situation at another public college in the same state.

Many state colleges, and some entire state systems, have reciprocity agreements with other states, in which students from those states pay in-state tuition. For example, Wisconsin residents going to school at state and community colleges in Minnesota pay in-state tuition rates, and vice versa.

Some reciprocity agreements are on a college-by-college rather than state-by-state basis. For instance, the University of Minnesota has made agreements with individual state colleges and universities in Utah, Colorado, Alaska, New Mexico, and several other states. The University of Minnesota charges residents of these states in-state tuition; in exchange, each of the schools in the other states offers Minnesota residents in-state tuition.

Solution 1: Call the agency that coordinates college financial aid programs for your home state. (You can get this number by calling the state department of education, the state office of higher education, and/or the financial aid office of any college in the state.) Ask which of the state's college financial aid programs, if any, provides aid to state residents who attend college out of state. Find out how to apply to any of these programs.

Also call the admissions office of each state or community college outside of your home state that seriously interests you. Ask to speak with an admissions representative; tell this person what state you live in, and ask if a reciprocity agreement exists which will permit you to pay in-state tuition. Also ask how that school defines in-state residency for tuition and financial aid purposes, and what you must do to be considered an in-state resident.

Solution 2: Most community colleges, and many state universities, will automatically award you in-state status for tuition purposes (and, in some cases, for financial aid purposes as well) if you use an off-campus mailing address within that state when you register for classes or apply for financial aid. You *may* therefore be able to register as an in-state student simply by moving to the appropriate state shortly before registration. You may also qualify for in-state tuition and financial aid after your first year, or the first time you register and apply for financial aid from an off-campus address within that state.

Solution 3: Move to the state in which you want to attend school. During the next year, work or do something else other than take classes. Then apply for admission and financial aid for the following year. In most cases you will be eligible for both in-state tuition and in-state financial aid.

If you move to another state for purposes other than attending college, or if your whole family moves to that state, you *still* may not qualify for in-state tuition and/or financial aid from that state until as much as a year has passed.

Some states require a waiting period before in-state status can take effect. One year is pretty standard, though it can be longer or much shorter.

Solution: Check with the college admissions office to find out exactly what the regulations are for qualifying for in-state tuition and/ or financial aid. If you feel it's appropriate, explain your particular situation and ask what your best course of action might be. Be sure to mention that your whole family has moved to that state, or that you have moved to the state for purposes other than attending college.

Your college may reduce your financial aid after your first year of college.

Each winter or spring, you will need to reapply for financial aid. At that time your college will reevaluate your financial situation and come up with an aid offer for the following academic year.

Your college has the right to reduce your financial aid if your family's financial circumstances have improved. However, if your family's finances remain about the same, your aid package should also remain substantially the same—in fact, it should be a little bigger, to allow for inflation. The makeup of the package (i.e., the amount in loans, the amounts in grants, etc.) should also be similar to the previous year's.

Solution: If you are offered an aid package that is poorer than the one you received last year, your parents should immediately speak to a financial aid officer about it, and firmly request specific and reasonable improvements.

However, they should also be prepared in the end to have to compromise, or even be told, "Sorry, take it or leave it."

Beware of advice from financial planners, or financial advice from anyone who is not very familiar with the range of federal, state,

college-based, and private financial aid programs available. These people may give you and your parents misleading or wholly incorrect advice—advice which could actually make you *ineligible* for financial aid, and cost you and your parents thousands of dollars in lost assistance.

All kind of people—bankers, tax preparers, accountants, professional financial planners, and authors of articles in magazines—claim to be experts on "paying for college." In fact, the vast majority of these people know little or nothing about college financial aid. What they *do* know about is investing, saving, and/or tax accounting. Typically, these folks have two messages:

(1) Save money, save money, and save more money.

(2) Invest your money wisely, in _____ [fill in the blank].

All of this is fine if your family is so well off that need-based financial aid is neither a possibility nor a necessity. But if you live in a low-, middle-, or even upper-middle-income family, these people's advice can be disastrous.

If you and your family save what you reasonably can for college without denying yourselves any necessities, you are planning for college properly. Financial aid will make up most or all of the difference between what college costs and what you can afford. But if you and your parents follow the advice of these "experts" and devote your lives to saving up enough money to pay the full cost of college, be assured that your college *will* expect you and your family to pay the full cost on your own.

Financial planners and accountants also frequently suggest to parents that they put some of their assets in their children's names, so that the earnings on those assets will be taxed at a lower rate. This is a fine idea *if* you don't plan to apply for financial aid. But if you do, this strategy could seriously reduce the amount of aid you are eligible for—or even make you ineligible entirely. See page 35 for details.

Solution: Beware of anyone who offers advice on paying for college who is not knowledgeable about financial aid. Such a person knows half the story at best.

A financial planner *may* be helpful if your parents have generous assets and/or incomes—large enough that need-based financial aid is out of the question. Even then, I strongly recommend that your parents work only with a planner who charges by the hour for his services—not one who earns a commission on what he sells. A planner who earns commissions has a powerful incentive to try to sell your parents investments or products.

Many families, of course, don't need a financial planner—just some good basic information. A good book on saving and investing for college is *Planning Now For College Costs* by Coopers and Lybrand (ASCU, 1988); it is available for $3 postpaid from Planning Now, Box 2155, Washington, DC 20013.

3

Registration and Scheduling

Lines to register and/or add and drop classes may be depressingly long.

Actually, at most colleges, registration lines have gotten dramatically shorter during the past decade. In fact, college administrations now have the knowledge and technology to reduce the waiting time in any registration line to ten minutes or less.

If you have to wait more than ten minutes to register, it is either because the computer system is temporarily down, or, more likely, because your college has decided that your time is not important. If you have to wait more than half an hour, your school has probably decided that *you* are of no importance.

Add/drop lines are another matter, however, because they are much more unpredictable. Expect a wait of up to twenty minutes; if you have to wait much longer, your college has planned or staffed its add/drop center inadequately.

Solution: Whenever possible, avoid in-person registration.

The vast majority of schools now permit mail registration (though sometimes this option is not available to new freshmen and transfer students). Indeed, you should have doubts about attending any college with more than five hundred students that does not offer registration by mail.

A few colleges now have the technology in place to permit students to register by computer and modem; doubtless many more will offer this option by the end of the decade. Registering by modem is not only faster than mail registration, but it enables you to find out which classes are already filled, to immediately select another course if the one you want is closed, and to confirm your registration on the spot. Contact your registration office for details. If you do not have a computer and modem of your own, ask if it is possible to use one of the campus computers to register.

It is always in your best interest to register as early as possible, so that you have the widest range of courses to choose from.

Adding and dropping courses can usually be done by mail or modem as well. I recommend using a modem whenever possible, and adding and dropping courses in person when it is not.

Adding and dropping courses by mail can be a bit risky. Keep the following items in mind:

(1) Many colleges charge partial tuition for courses not dropped by the first or second week of classes—or, in some cases, by the first day. If you drop a course by mail, make sure that your drop request arrives early enough to avoid extra charges.

(2) Adding courses by mail can be frustrating. If the course you want is closed, you won't get into it—and you won't learn that you didn't get into it until several days after you mailed your request. The only courses I would add by mail are those with no enrollment limit and those for which you have obtained the permission of the instructor.

Some colleges now permit students to register or add/drop by phone. Contact your registration office to see if this option is available.

If in-person registration (or add/drop) is your only or best option, but registering in person is quite difficult for you, you may have someone else do it for you. Write a short note that says, "I am unable to register in person and authorize ———— to appear on my behalf." Type or print your name, the date, your social security number, and your official student number (if different from your social security number). Sign the note and give it to the person who will register you or add/drop courses on your behalf.

Some or even all of the classes you want may be filled and closed, even if you register early.

Popular classes fill up very quickly. At large universities, some limited-enrollment classes may fill and close on the first or second day of registration.

Getting the classes you request depends a great deal on how your college prioritizes registrations. At schools that process registrations on a strictly first-come, first-served basis, registering as early as possible will all but ensure that you get the courses you want. Many colleges, however, process registrations according to class standing— that is, seniors and graduate students get the first pick of all courses, juniors' requests are processed next, sophomores' next, and freshmen's last. (Some colleges place the classes in a different order of priority. One school I know of gives freshmen third priority in registration and leaves the dregs for sophomores.)

Some colleges process registrations in a randomly determined priority based on students' social security numbers or the first letters of their last names—for example, registrations from students whose last name begins with G might be processed first, then the H's, and so on, with the E's last.

Solution 1: Once again, register absolutely as early as possible. Call the registration office halfway through the current term and find out the date on which registration for the following term will begin. If you will be a new freshman or transfer student, call the registration office as soon as you accept admission and find out the earliest day on which you can register; be sure to explain that you are a new freshman or transfer student.

At least a week before this date, pick up a class schedule for the following term from the registration office, or call and ask to have one mailed to you. Read the class schedule carefully from cover to cover and make your choices. Then make sure your registration is received on the first day of registration, or as soon thereafter as possible.

This works beautifully at colleges that register students on a first-come, first-served basis. If your school uses a different set of priorities, this approach will still help, but you will need to use the following strategy as well:

Solution 2: With few exceptions, you can get into any course on campus if you get the instructor's permission. This permission is not usually hard to obtain.

If a course or section that you want to take has a limited enrollment, ask for a Permission of Instructor form from your registration office. When signed by your instructor, this form authorizes your registration in her class *even if it is full and officially closed.* (Some schools don't use such a form, and simply leave a space on the registration form for the instructor's signature. In this case, just get a blank registration form.)

Then visit the instructor during her office hours, *preferably before registration for the following term begins* (or, if this is not possible, as soon afterward as you can). Bring with you the Permission of Instructor or registration form. Explain politely that you're extremely interested in the course and that you'd like to make sure that you get a place in it; then ask the instructor to sign your form.

About half of the teachers you talk to will immediately sign your form, and some will be impressed by your interest and assertiveness. The other half will say either, "I'm sorry, but I don't like to do end runs around the people in the registration office" or "Let's see what happens during the first week of the term." Respond to this by saying politely, "I understand. But would you be willing to put me on a waiting list for the course, so that if somebody drops out early in the term, I can take his or her place?" About half the time the instructor will agree to do so; but if she says, "Well, I haven't been keeping a waiting list," ask her to start one.

Do register for the courses as soon as possible. If you get into it, great. But if you don't, do not give up. *You still have a seventy-five percent chance of getting in.*

Show up early for the first class meeting, even though you are not yet officially registered in it. Sitting up front is a good idea. Bring your Permission of Instructor or registration form with you.

When the class is over, speak with the instructor again. Remind her of your earlier meeting; if she has already put you on a waiting list, remind her of this fact as well. Ask her if now she will be willing to authorize your registration in the course. About half the time this will do the trick.

But if she still says no, don't give up. Say, "May I sit in on the class for the first two weeks? If nobody has dropped out by the end of the second week, I'll stop coming." Most instructors will have no problem with this.

Keep coming to the class. Be early or on time, and sit near the front. You don't need to participate any more or differently than you normally would. Don't try to impress or flatter the teacher; this is unnecessary and sleazy. Just be yourself.

At the end of the second week, check with the instructor once again after class, and ask if she will now approve your registration. At this point, most teachers will, whether or not anybody has dropped the class. Most will also be impressed by your interest and stick-to-itiveness. (Just so you know, however, in ninety-six percent of all classes at least one student does drop out by the end of the second week.)

Important: be sure to check your class schedule to find out the last day on which you may add a course with the instructor's permission. Usually this is a week or two later than the last "regular" day to add courses. If you want to add a class after this deadline, you will need your dean's signature as well.

Courses constantly close, open, reclose, and reopen during registration. A class that is closed when you try to register for it may open up again five minutes later when a student drops it from his schedule. It may close again ten minutes after that, when another student signs up for it.

In other words, luck and timing often partly determine which classes you get and which ones you don't.

Solution 1: Instead of trusting to luck, follow the suggestions in the above section.

Solution 2: If a class you want is closed and you cannot get the instructor's permission to register for it, you can use this constant opening and closing in your favor.

Once per week, attempt to add the course you want, in the hope that you'll hit the timing right and make your request shortly after another student has dropped the course. If you have not gotten into the course by the time the new term begins, try to add it twice a day. Keep this up until you get into the course, or until the end of the add/drop period.

Courses and sections that are supposedly filled and closed may actually be open.

In or near your registration office, you will probably find posted a complete list of all courses for the current and/or upcoming term. When a course or section first fills up and closes during registration, the people in the registration office will either write "closed" or "full" next to the course title or section number on this list. They may even cross out the class or section. This notation will remain throughout registration and the add/drop period.

However, *any* closed classes may (and probably will) open up again when students drop it from their schedules. As I explained earlier, that class may reclose and reopen several more times by the end of the add/drop period. But the notation on the posted list will remain unchanged.

Solution: Always ignore any posted notices that claim a course is closed. Keep trying to register for it, and follow the other advice in this chapter.

Colleges usually cancel some courses during registration, and sometimes afterward. Occasionally they may even cancel courses at the first class meeting.

Classes are canceled at the last minute for a variety of reasons, but usually because few students have signed up for them.

The courses most likely to be canceled are junior- or senior-level classes with highly focused and specialized subject matter. Introductory courses are rarely canceled.

Solution: Be prepared for cancellations. When you choose your courses for the term, always pick at least a few backups. If a course you signed up for does get canceled, replace it as quickly as you can with something else you genuinely want to take.

Colleges sometimes *add* courses during or just before registration as well. Often new sections of courses may be added as late as the first week of the term.

Sometimes instructors are late in providing the registration office with course information, and their courses have to be announced later. Sometimes new instructors are hired at the last minute. And sometimes a department will add one or more new sections of a popular course when it becomes clear that the demand for it far exceeds the supply of available spaces.

Solution 1: Notices of any new courses and sections will be posted at the registration office. Sometimes special notices are put up, but usually the new additions are simply written in by hand on the posted list of courses, under the appropriate department's name. You may wish to visit the registration office every week or two during registration to see if anything interesting has been added.

If you simply cannot get into a course that you want, check each day during the first week of the term to see if a new section of the course has been added.

Solution 2: Registration offices at some colleges publish supplemental course schedule information, and distribute this information to all students. Read any such supplement carefully.

You may be refused entrance to a course even though you have obtained permission from the instructor to enroll in it.

This is not as harrowing as it sounds, and it's easy to deal with. Usually one of two things has happened: (1) a registration staff person failed to notice that you obtained the instructor's permission, or (2) the registration computer is (improperly) programmed not to admit more than a certain number of students to the course, even if you have the instructor's permission.

Solution: Go to your dean and explain the situation. Bring with you all appropriate documents (the list of courses the registration office assigned you, etc.). Usually the dean can solve the problem for you with a simple phone call. At worst, he'll ask you to obtain your instructor's signature a second time and then reregister.

You may need to make major changes in your schedule during the first week or two of the term.

All sorts of unexpected things can happen at the beginning of the term: A course may prove to be much harder than you expected; a different (and far less interesting) instructor may end up teaching it; the course might be moved to a building across campus, making it impossible to get to in time; the teacher, who was so friendly and helpful in her office, may turn out to be an ogre in class; the course may be canceled completely; or your work schedule or personal obligations may change significantly.

Solution: Expect surprises. Be ready and willing to add and/or drop courses—and even rearrange your whole schedule—any time during the first week or two of the term. If and when you realize that a change is necessary, make it as soon as you can.

You may be forced unexpectedly to change to a higher- or lower-level math or writing course during the first two weeks of the term.

Before your first college term begins, your school will probably evaluate your math and writing skills and decide which class in each subject is appropriate for you. Its evaluation may be based on a placement exam, SAT or ACT scores, Achievement Test scores, your high school academic record, or some combination of these.

These evaluations are far from foolproof, however; about ten percent of the time they prove inaccurate. Many math and writing teachers therefore do their own evaluations of their students' skills at the beginning of the term. If your instructor believes that you're in too difficult or too easy a course, he will ask, encourage, or order you to switch to one more appropriate for you.

Solution: If your teacher tells you that you should be in a harder or easier course, believe him—he knows what he's talking about. Indeed, following his advice may make your whole college career easier. Drop his course and add the new course that he suggests.

If all the sections of this more appropriate math or writing class are full, or if none of the sections that are open fit into your schedule, see your dean. Explain that you were initially placed in the wrong class, and that getting into the right class now seems impossible. Ask the dean if she can get you into one of the closed sections. Also feel free to talk with instructors who teach sections of the course you need, and ask them to let you join their classes. Be sure to get a signature authorizing your registration in the course. Another possibility is putting off the class until the following term, when you will be able to pick the section and teacher you prefer. However, you may need to bolster your math or writing skills now in order to use them in your other classes; in this case, you are probably better off taking the course this term.

If you realize *on your own* that you're in way over your head—even if your teacher doesn't—it is imperative that you switch to a lower-level class. If there is no room in any section of this class that fits your schedule, follow the advice above.

The scheduling computer may screw up your registration. It may even refuse to let you register at all.

This happens, on average, once in each student's college career.

One of the most common computer errors is refusing to permit a student to register because of a nonexistent academic hold on her record, or an equally nonexistent outstanding debt.

Solution: Go to your dean with any and all pertinent documents. He'll fix everything up quickly, usually with just a phone call or two.

If your registration is postponed because of a computer error, you may wish to say to the dean, "Because of the delay caused by this error, I may not be able to get all the courses I wanted. Would you be willing to sign me into a course if it has closed out?" The dean is under no obligation to do this, but he may feel enough guilt or pity to do it for you.

If you do not have alternate times, sections, and classes in mind when registering or adding classes, you may wind up with few or none of the courses you want.

There is considerable variation in how course-registration computer programs work. At some schools, if you try to register for a class or section that has filled up, you simply won't get that class or section. At others, the computer is programmed to try to register you in a different section of that same class. At still others, you have the option of listing second and third choices; if your first choice is not available, the computer will try to give you one of your alternate choices. Under any of these arrangements, however, you still may end up with fewer courses or credits than you want or need, or even with no classes at all.

Solution 1: Again, decide which teachers, courses, and sections you want, then secure each instructor's permission to register in his or her course.

I suggest following one or both of these suggestions as well:

Solution 2: If your college will allow you to list alternate courses on your registration form, do so. Pick these as carefully as you do your first choices. List as many alternates as the form will allow, in order of preference; however, *only include as alternates courses and sections that genuinely appeal to you.*

If your registration form has no place for listing alternate courses, make up a list of alternates anyway, in order or preference, for your possible use later. If you need to add and/or drop courses, simply refer to this list.

Solution 3: Register for more courses than you actually plan to take—then drop one of them later, either after you receive your schedule or once the term begins.

For example, if you plan to take three classes, register for four. List all four courses as your primary choices. You may also list alternates as well. If you get into all four courses, great; pick the three you want the most, and drop the fourth. Or, better yet, leave all four in your schedule. During the first week of classes, go to all four and get a feel for each; *then* pick the three you like best and drop the fourth.

If you only get three of the four classes you asked for, you still wind up with three classes that you wanted. And even if you only get one or two of the courses you requested, you probably did better than you would have if you had only tried to register for your three top choices. Try to get teachers' permission to register for the remaining classes.

Important: Some colleges set a limit on the number of courses or credits you may register for without the permission of your dean. *If you exceed this number, your registration may not be processed.* Before you register, call your registration office to find out the maximum, and do not exceed it.

You will also need to be careful about money. Registering for an extra course may mean a higher tuition bill. Most colleges charge the same tuition for twelve to sixteen (or even eighteen) credits; some, though, charge a flat rate per credit or course, particularly for part-time students. However, most colleges will permit you to pay your tuition bill one to seven weeks after you register; so you can register for the overload, then drop the additional course just before your tuition bill is due and pay only for those courses remaining in your schedule.

In course schedules and your college's catalog, some courses will be listed in departments where you might not expect to find them.

If you're looking for a course in photography, it might be offered by any of these departments: art, communications, journalism, graphic design, humanities, visual studies—or even, at one college, drama. A class in business writing might be offered through the department of business, communications, composition, English, literature, rhetoric, or writing.

In fact, just figuring out what a department might call itself is sometimes difficult. What most colleges call their drama department is called by various schools the department of theater, performance studies, and stage. Other colleges combine drama with other fields to create the joint departments of inter-arts, dance and drama, literature and drama, and film and theater.

There's one other twist to all this: At some large universities, two similar or virtually identical courses may be offered by two different departments in two different schools within that university. For example, both the college of business and the school of journalism might offer a course in publication design.

Solution: Read (or at least skim) *all* the course listings in your college catalog and each course schedule. Check out every department and every item. You'll find some good courses that you might otherwise have missed; you'll stumble upon some items in unlikely places; and you'll discover some potentially fascinating courses that you didn't consider before or didn't even know existed.

As for two similar courses offered by different departments, check out both teachers and both courses; then pick the class you find most appealing.

If you have any outstanding debt to any office or division of your college—even ten cents owed to the library—you may not be permitted to register.

Colleges can be ruthless about this. But since eighty percent of students' outstanding debts are parking and library fines, rarely is there a great deal of money at stake.

Solution: At least ten days before you register, pay off all your debts to the college, including any overdue bills and any parking and library fines. If there is a dispute over how much money you owe, resolve it before you register; if it is unresolvable now and the amount of money in question is fifty dollars or less, pay it off so that you can register, and resolve it later. Keep in mind that there can be a time lag of a couple of days between the time you pay everything off and the time the computer clears you to register.

It is also a good idea to call the registration office a few days before you register, even if you have no outstanding debts. Ask the staff to pull up your record on the computer and make sure that you are cleared to register for the following term. If there is a problem of any kind, you can take care of it immediately—before registration begins.

You may be forced to declare a major on registration forms long before you are ready to make an intelligent choice.

Some colleges' registration forms will ask you to list your major, even if you're a first-semester freshman—and if you don't fill in something, your registration may not be processed.

Solution: Always fill in the blank for a major, and any other blank you're instructed to fill in. If you haven't decided on a major yet, write in the major that currently most interests you. If you have no idea what your major might be at all, pick one at random. *You will be under no obligation to actually major in this subject.* All you are doing is satisfying the temporary needs of the registration computer.

Beware of any waiting list kept by registration staff people. Chances are it will be completely ignored, and very possibly thrown away.

Instructors often keep waiting lists for their courses. These are the only course waiting lists you want to be on. Any other waiting lists for courses are useless.

At the great majority of colleges, registration offices simply do not keep waiting lists for any courses. At a few schools, however, for reasons I cannot fathom, staffpeople *do* keep waiting lists, which they do absolutely nothing with. I have seen people at registration take downs students' names and phone numbers on a waiting list, then throw the list into a wastebasket.

Solution: If you cannot get an instructor's permission to enroll in her course, ask her to put you on her own waiting list. But don't bother with any waiting list kept by anyone else: It's a waste of time.

Waiting lists *for admission to a college* are a different matter. These are kept by the admissions office, and they are real and legitimate.

Your college's registration computer may not give you enough time between classes to get from one to the next.

Many registration programs give students a set amount of time between classes—usually ten to thirty minutes—no matter how physically close or far apart those classes may be.

This can be a problem especially at large universities, where getting from one end of campus to another can easily take half an hour—longer in bad weather. It is a still bigger problem at universities that have two or three campuses in the same city, with service between the campuses provided by shuttle buses. At one of these schools, you may be given half an hour between classes—but the first shuttle bus that leaves after your first class ends may not get you to your next class until ten minutes after it starts.

Solution: When you first plan your schedule for the term, get out a campus map (and, if need be, campus bus schedules). Plot the location of each class. As you pick your courses, figure out how long it will take to get from one to the next *under the least favorable conditions.* Allow extra time for bad weather.

If you will need to take a bus between classes, check the bus schedules. Make sure that you can *easily* get from one class to the next via bus; again, allow some extra time for bad weather and late buses.

If, when you get your official schedule from the registration office, you were given any sections or courses other than your original choices, get out your campus map and bus schedules once more. Make sure that getting from class to class on time is physically possible. If it's not, change your schedule.

Avoid the following under all circumstances:

• Classes scheduled close enough together that you have to hurry from one to the next. This leaves you no time to stay after your first class and speak to your instructor, should you need to. It also leaves you no leeway should the first class run overtime, and no slack for delays caused by bad weather.

• Any bus that you have to catch immediately after class, or that arrives close to the beginning of the next. Whenever circumstances are less than perfect, you're going to be late for the second class—and few teachers consider "the bus was late" to be an adequate excuse more than once or twice during the term.

The standard schedule of fourteen to sixteen credits is a heavy load.

A typical full-time course load of fourteen to sixteen credits requires thirty to forty-five hours per week of study (including time spent in class), and fifty to seventy hours per week before midterm and final exams. A single four-credit course typically requires a total of eight to twelve hours of work per week, including class time, and twelve to sixteen hours before midterms and finals.

These figures will probably prove true for you no matter how brilliant you are. It's possible to reduce your studying time by perhaps fifteen percent with careful planning and scheduling, other time management techniques, and first-rate study skills; but no matter how you look at it, college will take up a great deal of your time.

Solution: Don't overcommit yourself. If you're not careful, it's extremely easy to take on more than you can handle.

Before you register for the upcoming term, carefully consider all your commitments and how much time you will need to spend on each. Remember to include time for travel to and from school (and between classes), leisure time, time for necessary tasks such as laundry and shopping, time spent with your family and/or your boyfriend or girlfriend, sufficient time for meals and sleep, etc. If you're honest with yourself, you'll see that there isn't a lot of time to spare.

While you should of course base any decision on your own needs and habits, keep these generalities in mind:

• If you are a full-time student taking fourteen to sixteen credits, do not work more than about ten hours a week at a job; if you are taking more than sixteen credits, don't work at all. If you exceed any of these limits, you will almost certainly find yourself with too much to do and not enough time to do it.

• If you need to work ten to fifteen hours a week, take no more than three classes or twelve credits per term. Twelve credits is still considered full-time at almost all schools.

• If you must work full-time, taking one class per term is plenty; two is difficult; and three is usually impossible.

• If you work half-time, you can probably handle two classes (up to eight credits)—three (nine to twelve credits) at the absolute outside.

One other note: At some colleges, a standard full-time course load consists of three five-credit classes; at others, four four-credit classes; and at still others, five three-credit classes. In general, I have found that five three-credit classes require several more hours of work per week than four four-credit courses, which in turn require several more hours of work each week than three five-credit courses. Plan your schedule accordingly.

If you do not follow your college's graduation procedures on time and to the letter, you may not be permitted to graduate when planned.

Most schools have a specific procedure students must go through in their final term in order to graduate. This often involves filing a graduation application and/or paying a graduation fee. It also means paying any outstanding fines or bills. If you do not take care of every item in this procedure, your graduation may be delayed until the following term.

Solution: At the beginning of the term in which you expect to graduate, call both the registration office *and* the office of your dean. In each case, explain that you expect to graduate at the end of the term, and ask what forms you will need to fill out and what other tasks you must complete in order to graduate on time. Find out the deadline for each task.

If the dean's office and the registration office give you slightly different procedures, follow both sets. The registration office has probably given you the university-wide procedures, and the dean has probably informed you of the procedures for your particular school or college within the university.

Be sure to complete each required task by its deadline. To ensure that all goes smoothly, take one additional step: One month before the term ends, call or visit the registration office. Ask the staff there to pull up your record on their computer and make sure that everything is in order for your graduation. Have them check to see that all your bills and fines have been paid, that all necessary courses have been completed (or will be completed by the end of the term), and that all required forms have been filed. This step will head off any potential problems and ensure that you graduate when you expect to.

If your graduation *is* delayed for any *nonacademic* reason, you may still claim that you have completed your degree in résumés, letters to employers, etc. What's important to employers is that you have fulfilled all the academic requirements for the degree, not whether or not you've been through a ceremony or received a special piece of paper.

4

Rules and Regulations

Teachers, administrators, and staff people often do not fully understand college rules, no matter how much they may think and insist that they do.

Most colleges have an untold number of regulations and policies. Many are quite complex and detailed, and many have exceptions. Some of these rules change often.

Furthermore, sometimes two or more conflicting rules may be in force simultaneously. For instance, freshmen beginning college in the fall of 1992 or thereafter may have different graduation requirements than freshmen who entered college before that time.

The result is that many people do not fully understand all the nuances of all the rules—including people such as advisors and instructors.

Solution: Virtually all of the rules and regulations that apply to you will be included in your college's catalog. Consider this catalog as a standard reference tool.

Each year, when your college's new catalog is published, get a copy, read it carefully, save it, and refer to it as necessary. When you have a question about a rule, check for the answer in the current catalog first.

You can usually get a copy of the current catalog through the admissions office. When you get the current year's edition, also find out when the next edition will be published, and make a note to pick one up as soon as it is available. Catalogs are usually free, though some schools charge a few dollars per copy.

Each academic department also has its own regulations, which apply to its courses, major, minor, and other departmental matters. If you plan to major, minor, or take more than a few courses in a certain department, ask the department secretary for a copy of the department handbook—or, if there is no handbook, for printed information describing the department's policies, procedures, and programs. Read this information carefully as well; save it and refer to it when you need to.

Whenever anything an administrator or staffperson tells you conflicts with what the current college catalog or current department handbook says, bring this conflict to the person's attention *and ask him to check the rule for you.* If, after checking, he still claims the catalog or handbook is incorrect, ask him to explain the discrepancy. Find out if the rule has changed—and, if so, when. Also find out if there are any exceptions. (Note: When information in a department handbook conflicts with information in your college bulletin, believe the department handbook; however, do confirm it with the department secretary.)

Another good—but somewhat less reliable—source of information on college rules is the student handbook which many colleges give to their new students. If you receive a student handbook when you first enroll, read it and save it. If you are not given a new handbook when it comes out each summer or fall, request one from the orientation or student affairs office.

If something your student handbook says contradicts what the college catalog, a department handbook, or an administrator or staff person says, check the rule.

The ultimate authorities on most college rules and policies are the deans. If you have a question about any college regulation, call the appropriate dean's office. The dean's secretary should be able to help you; if she can't, the dean or assistant dean can.

Colleges may suddenly change their rules on you.

So may governments, of course, although colleges often give less advance warning.

Solution: If a rule that affects you seems to have changed, ask about it. If it turns out that it has changed, ask to see a copy of it in writing. Once you have a copy, read it over carefully to make sure that you understand it completely and that it is being correctly applied to you. Hang on to your copy of the new rule indefinitely.

If you are told that the rule has *not* changed, firmly but politely insist that things used to be different. Ask the person to check the rule; if she refuses or continues to say that the rule has not changed, ask to see the rule in writing. If you like, bring her your college catalog or the appropriate department handbook, show her what the rule actually says, and ask her to explain the discrepancy. If need be, speak to her superior.

Changes in rules covering everyday life (dorm selection, parking, social events, etc.) and support services (registration, the library, the college health clinic, etc.) usually affect everyone. However, changes in graduation requirements, majors, and most other academic matters do *not* apply to everyone.

In general, *the academic regulations and policies that were in effect at the time you first enrolled at your college remain in effect* for you *until you graduate—even if those rules are changed radically or multiple times.* This remains true even if you take a leave of absence, or drop out and later reenroll.

For instance, when you first enroll, if Biology 101 is the only biology course required for graduation, that requirement will not change *for you*, even if, a month later, the college changes its policy and requires Biology 101, 102, and 110 for graduation.

There is one exception to all of this: Changes in a particular major or minor *may* apply to you if you have not yet declared that major or minor. Check with your dean's office for details.

If any academic policy does change, and it is unclear how or whether it affects you, contact your dean's office for an explanation. Explain clearly when you first enrolled in the college and ask whether the change applies to you. With few exceptions, it should not; if you are told that it does, ask the person to double check.

Once you have a clear answer from the dean's office, believe it. If any other administrator or staffperson contradicts it, politely correct him and suggest that he contact the dean's office if he has any doubts.

Many college rules and regulations have nothing to do with education, and are made purely for political reasons.

If you are required to pass a geography course in order to graduate, it may be because the college faculty believes strongly that geography is an essential part of a college education; but it may also be because a past president of the college was an ex–geography instructor. If you have to pass an exam on your state's constitution to get your bachelor's degree, it's not necessarily because teachers and administrators think this is important, but perhaps because the school had to require it to appease lawmakers and receive state funding.

Colleges and universities are not above or exempt from the bizarre and petty forces of politics. As a result, some of your college's rules may not make much sense, and some may hinder rather than support your education.

Solution: An exception can be made to almost any college policy, procedure, or regulation with the appropriate person's permission. Indeed, part of any administrator's job is to make an exception to the rules when one is warranted. Deans are usually the people with the ultimate authority to make exceptions.

Challenging a rule just because it's generally silly or senseless won't work. However, if you can show that your own situation is unusual, and that therefore a certain rule should not apply to you, you can often convince your dean or another administrator to bend that rule for you. Here's what to do:

Make an appointment with the appropriate person. Arrive on time; being neatly dressed and groomed helps a bit. Throughout your meeting, be polite, calm, and respectful.

Begin by explaining the rule in question and how it works. Then explain why you believe that *in your particular case* the rule does not or should not apply. Present specific information and evidence to support your explanation.

For instance, if your college requires that all students take at least two terms of a foreign language to graduate, but you already speak fluent German and French as well as English, you might say to your dean, "I agree that it's important that students be encouraged to be at least bilingual, if not trilingual. But I'm already fluent in three different languages. To show you, I've translated the first two pages of the college catalog into both French and German. I think my situation is unusual, and instead of learning yet another language I'd like to use those ten credits to explore some subjects in the sciences that have always intrigued me."

Important: *Do not try to argue the merits of the rule itself.* This simply won't work, no matter how daft the rule may be.

Living on campus does not exempt you from any of the local, state, or federal laws.

Like it or not, as a college student you are not only a part of your college community, but also a part of the town or city in which the college is located. Most or all of that community's standards will be applied to you—and enforced by the police. These standards govern, among other things, drinking, drug use, driving, parking, parties, and rowdy behavior in general.

Solution: Be careful and discreet—just as careful and discreet as you would need to be if you lived off campus.

You may be required to pay a hefty student health fee each term. However, this fee may provide very limited health care coverage.

Most colleges have an on-campus health clinic which provides routine medical care, medical counseling, and related services (birth control, etc.) to students, usually at little or no charge. Many schools charge a health fee each term to support this clinic.

A few schools take a different approach: They require all students (or all full-time students) to have health insurance coverage, and offer students at least one such plan. Some colleges and universities charge a health fee *and* require that students own health insurance.

Unfortunately, neither the student health clinic nor a college-sponsored health insurance plan may provide you with the medical coverage you need. With few exceptions, student health fees do not cover hospitalization, operations, or most forms of nonroutine medical treatment. College-sponsored health insurance plans also may provide very limited coverage: They may lapse during summers and/or school vacations, they may have a very low upper limit for coverage, and/or they may not cover both major medical and hospitalization expenses.

Solution: When you first enroll, find out exactly what coverage your health fee provides and whether a health insurance plan is required or available. You and/or your parents should be mailed detailed information on the subject; if you are not, call the admissions office or college health service and ask for it.

If the health fee does not provide comprehensive coverage, including both hospitalization and major medical, *for twelve full months per year*, you will need to purchase insurance or HMO coverage.

Health insurance plans offered by colleges range from excellent to awful, and from inexpensive to outrageous. You or your parents should study any such plan carefully, and compare it with other available plans. Although you may be required to pay a regular health fee, *you do not have to purchase college-sponsored health insurance.* You always have the option of buying coverage elsewhere.

In many cases, the best and simplest thing for your parents to do is retain the insurance or HMO coverage they already have on you. Most HMOs and insurance companies allow families to continue providing coverage for their children until they complete college.

Most colleges charge several other fees each term as well: student activity fees, general fees, bus fees, etc.

These fees are simply surcharges that colleges add on to the costs of tuition, room, and board to raise extra money. Often they are minimal, but at some colleges they can total several hundred dollars per term.

Solution: Find out exactly what these fees are and how much they run when you first decide to apply. Complete information is available in college catalogs and course schedules, or by calling the college registration office. Be sure to include these fees in your calculations when you consider financial aid, expenses, and the amount of money you will need to earn and save.

Many colleges also charge fees for parking, transferring credits, getting a student ID, and even graduating.

Nearly every college raises extra money by nickel and diming students, though each school has its own variations. Some of these include fees to:

- get or replace an ID card
- park a car on campus
- transfer in credits from other schools

- send out a transcript
- send out a dossier to potential employers and/or graduate programs
- participate in science labs
- use the college's mainframe computer and/or a computer network
- eat or live off campus
- graduate

Solution: Same as above.

You may be required to know how to use a computer to graduate, or to be admitted. You may even be required to know how to use a particular brand of computer and some of its related software.

Since colleges now use computers in so many of their courses, and since so many businesses and organizations in the outside world now use them as well, many schools make "computer literacy" a graduation requirement. Some, mostly institutes of science and technology, require it for admission. And a few insist that you know how to use a particular make of computer—usually IBM or Macintosh—before college begins. These schools will expect you to be ready, willing, and able to start using their computers and programs from your first day as a student.

Solution: Schools that require computer literacy for admission will clearly say so in their admissions material, and/or their catalogs. Read this material and these catalogs carefully.

If you lack the computer skills necessary for admission, *learn them* as soon as possible, because you will surely need them from the first day of your first term. Your options for learning these skills include:

(1) Signing up for a computer course as part of your high school studies.

(2) Taking a weekend or evening class in computing through a local community education program. Such programs are offered by public school systems, colleges, technical and vocational schools, museums, and other organizations. These courses typically carry no academic credit and are very reasonably priced. Computing courses are also offered through colleges for college credit, but they are

usually far more expensive. (You may, however, want to take a computing course for credit, then transfer in the credits and apply them toward your degree.)

(3) Taking a summer school course in computing.

If at all possible, learn on IBM PCs, IBM clones, or Macintoshes, since these are by far the most commonly used personal computers on college campuses.

If, as part of a college application, you are asked whether or not you have certain computer skills, answer honestly; but if you do not yet have those skills, add a phrase such as "I am currently taking a course that teaches these skills," "I have enrolled in a course on this subject," "I will take a course on this subject during the upcoming summer," etc.

You may be required to *buy* a computer and peripherals when you first enroll—even if you already own a computer.

Many colleges have standardized their computer networks and software. As a student, you may be expected to own the brand of computer and peripherals that your college uses.

Solution: Don't go out and buy a computer or computer system for college until you know exactly where you'll be going to school and exactly what system it uses.

When you first decide which schools to apply to, call up each college's admissions office and ask these questions:

- Do you require all students to buy or own personal computers?

- If so, what brand and model do you require?

- What peripherals and software must students also own?

- How much will all of this cost, including tax?

- Are the computers, peripherals, and software available through the college? Is there a student discount? Can these items be paid for through an installment plan?

- If owning a computer is not required, what computing facilities are available on campus for students to use? During what hours are these facilities open? How many personal computers, all told, are available for general student use?

If your school does require you to own a computer, remember to include the costs associated with it in your financial planning—and, if you will be applying for financial aid, in your aid application.

Some colleges will not allow you to transfer in certain courses. Some may not allow you to transfer in *any* courses from certain schools or programs.

Colleges and universities can sometimes be very picky about what they will accept for transfer credit. Usually they will only accept courses taken for academic credit at accredited colleges and universities.

Many schools will also limit or refuse to accept transfer credit for courses taken outside North America; for courses passed with grades lower than C or C − (B or B − for graduate credit); or for remedial or very basic courses such as Introduction to College Math, Study Skills, or Refresher English. Some colleges set a strict limit on the number of transfer credits that can be applied toward graduation, and/or toward a particular major or minor.

Some specialized colleges—particularly art schools, music conservatories, and institutes of technology—may refuse to transfer in courses in their area of specialty that were not taken at a similar specialized institution. For example, an art college may not allow you to transfer in the Introduction to Sculpture class you took at Cuyahoga Community College—but it *would* let you transfer in a class with the identical title from the Cleveland Institute of Art.

A very few colleges and programs will not accept any transfer credits at all.

Solution: Knowing how much transfer credit you can or will receive can make a huge difference in your college career. Transfer credits can cut terms or even years off the amount of time you need to complete your degree. They can also cut thousands—even tens of thousands—of dollars off your college costs. Because of all this, knowing in advance what courses you can transfer may affect which college you choose to attend.

If you are planning to transfer to another school, or if you have already earned some college credits at another college, or if you plan to take some classes at another college in the future, do not automatically assume that all your courses will be transferred in.

When you apply to any college, either as a freshman or a transfer student, make sure that you send the admissions office a transcript from every college where you have previously completed courses. Once you are offered admission, call up your admissions representative; if you have no official admissions representative, any rep in the admissions office will do. Ask her to pull your file, look at the transcripts, and tell you which of your previous college credits will probably transfer and which ones probably will not.

Since the final decision on the transfer of credits is not always made by the admissions office, what the admissions rep tells you will not be legally binding. But admissions representatives know from experience what their colleges usually accept and what they usually don't, so a rep's educated guess will be very close to the mark.

If your admissions rep refuses to make even a guess for you, ask her to refer you to someone who can. Then take your inquiry to that staffperson or administrator.

The purpose of all this is to avoid any nasty surprises after you have enrolled. If you have completed fifty college credits elsewhere, you do not want to find out after the fall term has begun that only four of these credits will transfer in.

Some schools will not make an official decisions on the transfer of your prior credit until after you have accepted admission and enrolled. This is fine, so long as you have gotten an informal assessment of your transfer credits prior to enrolling. If the actual number of credits transferred differs significantly from this informal assessment, something is wrong; bring the matter to your dean.

If you are already enrolled in a degree program at a college and plan to take some college credits elsewhere, check with your registration office before that study elsewhere begins. Explain exactly what and where you plan to study, when you plan to do it, and how many credits you expect to earn. *Make sure in advance that these credits will be accepted toward your degree.*

College catalogs usually describe most (but not always all) of each schools' regulations on the transfer of credits.

Some colleges will permit you to transfer in credit for previous "life experience": certain employment, volunteer work, self-directed study, non-credit classes, etc. Check with your dean or the admissions office for details.

The only transcripts any college will accept as legitimate are those sent directly to it from high schools and other colleges.

These are known as *official transcripts*. A transcript that you send yourself or have handled first is an *unofficial transcript*—and, from colleges' point of view, is meaningless.

Solution: Whenever any school requests a transcript, send an official one. High schools usually send transcripts at no charge; colleges charge one to four dollars per transcript.

Some schools still have curfews.

Most colleges have dropped these. Some still have them in their regulations, but never enforce them. However, some other schools still do enforce curfews, at least some of the time for some of their students (most often freshmen and/or women).

Solution: If a college does have a curfew, it will usually be noted in its catalog, under the section entitled "Student Life" or "Regulations for Students." This curfew may or may not be enforced.

On your all-important campus visit (see pages 3–7 for details), ask the dorm representative and a couple of dorm residents about curfews. They will let you know exactly how things actually work (as opposed to what the official regulation might be).

If you choose to attend a college that does enforce a curfew, your best solution is to live off campus, where campus curfews have no effect.

5

Parking and Transportation

At many colleges, finding a convenient parking spot, or even any parking spot, is often impossible.

Many colleges have a serious shortage of parking spaces. You can't fix the shortage, of course, but you can make things much easier on yourself.

Solution 1: If you are willing to do a little bit of walking—say, up to a quarter or a third of a mile—you can find a regular place to park on or near virtually any college campus in the country (except in Manhattan).

Before the term begins—or, if necessary, early one morning or late one evening once the term has started—take a leisurely drive around the campus. Bring a map of the campus with you. (One should appear in your school's schedule of classes for the term, as well as in its annual catalog. You can also get a map from your college's public relations office, or from the campus police.) Make a note of where all the campus parking lots are in relation to where you need to be. Make a special note of those lots which are at or near the edge of the campus, but which are within a five- or ten-minute walk of where you want to get to. These lots will be your best bets for on-campus parking: They're far enough away that they won't always be jammed, yet sufficiently close in that you can easily walk the rest of the way to your destination. Also note the location and cost of any pay lots on campus.

Next, check out all the on-campus streets. Note which ones permit parking, and what restrictions on hours or length of time apply.

Also take note of which campus lots and streets have meters, how long those meters run for, and how much they cost.

Now that you've scoped out everything on campus, take another short drive on the streets immediately surrounding it. Completely circle the campus, and check out every public street that runs nearby. *Your best bets for parking are usually public streets a few blocks from the edge of campus.* Spaces are almost always available, and parking is usually free.

If the streets close to campus have meters, and/or if parking on these streets is restricted, expand your circle a bit wider. Note where the meters and/or restrictions end, and plan to park just beyond them. If meters are completely unavoidable, note how long they run for and how much they cost.

Pick one slightly out-of-the-way on-campus lot and two or three off-campus areas as your standard parking territories. When you get to school, try the on-campus lot first. If it's full, don't waste your time driving around and hoping for a miracle; head straight for one of your designated off-campus parking areas.

Within a week or two after the term begins, you will know all the traffic and parking patterns around campus. You'll know when your on-campus lot is most likely to have a space, and when you'll need to park off campus. And you won't have to spend any time hunting and hoping for a prime parking space to appear magically.

Solution 2: If your school has satellite parking lots, and shuttle buses that run between the lots and campus, use them. Finding a parking space at one of these lots is never a problem. However, be sure to find out exactly when the shuttle buses run—and when they start and stop running each day of the week. You don't want to have to hitch a ride just to get to your car.

Solution 3: Parking is almost always easiest to find early in the morning (before 7:30 or 8:00 A.M.) and after three in the afternoon. If possible, get to campus early, park, and use your extra time to read, study, exercise in the gym, have breakfast, or just relax. Another option: Schedule some or all of your classes for afternoons and/or evenings.

Solution 4: Use public transportation. Taking the bus, subway, or train not only gets rid of all your on-campus parking problems, but can actually save you time as well. When you take public transportation, you can use the time to study, read, or listen to taped lectures as you travel; when you drive, you have to pay attention to the road.

Solution 5: Most colleges have a pay lot in or near the center of campus. This lot is open to anyone, costs fifty cents to a dollar per hour, and is rarely full. Consider this your emergency lot. When you're running late or need to get close to the center of campus in a hurry, use this lot and pay for the privilege. In tight situations, it's worth the money.

Campus police may be fanatical about giving parking tickets for even the smallest infractions.

College police are far quicker to spot violations and issue tickets than regular city and town police. Furthermore, while you can sometimes buck administrators, teachers, advisors, and deans, you cannot buck the parking police. You can appeal an on-campus parking citation (call the campus police to ask how), but it's usually a lost cause, because the appeal will be heard not by a court of law, but by a college official.

Solution: Learn to expect no mercy when it comes to parking violations. Follow the regulations as much as you can; when you get a ticket, pay it. If you have any question about parking regulations, ask the campus police.

Some colleges will not allow you to keep a car on campus at all.

With few exceptions, the only schools that have such a rule are liberal arts colleges in small towns, particularly those in the Midwest. If keeping a car on campus is important to you, find out what the regulations are before you accept admission (and perhaps before you even apply) to any small-town liberal arts college. But even if parking on campus is not permitted, you still have these options:

Solution 1: Park your car just beyond the campus border on a public street. Use the suggestions earlier in this chapter to find parking spots near your school.

Solution 2: Get a two-wheeled motorized vehicle. Some schools ban on-campus cars and trucks, but will allow you to keep a motorcycle, motor scooter, and/or moped on campus. Check with the campus police to see what the college's regulations allow.

Campus buses (including shuttle buses serving outlying parking lots) may run infrequently or not at all in the evenings, on weekends, and/or during vacations. Service may also be cut back during exam week.

Solution: Get a schedule for every bus line you are likely to use. Printed schedules are usually available in the student center; if they aren't, call the bus system office (or, if there is no such office, the campus police) to ask for running times. Keep schedule information handy at all times.

Toward the end of the term, check to find out if, when, and how schedules will change in the days to come.

Schedules may change from term to term. Be sure to get new schedules at the beginning of each new term.

Campus buses will not always run on time, especially in large cities.

Solution: Don't take the bus that arrives just in time for your class; take the earlier one. In bad weather, take the bus before that.

In general, give yourself at least twenty minutes after a bus's official arrival time to get to class. In bad weather, give yourself thirty or forty. Be prepared for delays; during bad weather, expect them.

Campus buses may be overcrowded. There may sometimes be no room to get on at all.

Crowded buses are understandable and often unavoidable; but buses too crowded to board are the result of poor planning by your college.

Solution: If a bus is too full to board, write down the number of the bus, the time it drove by, and the time you finally got to school. If you missed all or part of a class, write that down, too.

Then complain! The person to approach is the dean of students. Either write the dean a firm, polite letter or make an appointment to meet him or her in person.

In the letter or at the appointment, explain exactly what happened. Include the time of day and the number of the bus. If you missed part or all of a class as a result, say so; include the title of the course and the name of the instructor. Add a couple of sentences such as these: "It disturbs me that the campus bus service, which is designed to get me to class, instead forced me to miss my class. As it is currently being run, the campus bus service is interfering with my education." Suggest the following solution: more buses, and more frequent runs.

Your complaint alone may not change things—but remember that other people were probably unable to board that bus, too, and some of them will complain as well. Your collective voice may well cause the powers that be to improve bus service.

You may be required to pay a bus fee each term, even if you never ride campus buses.

Some colleges provide bus service to students at no charge; some charge each rider a fee; some sell weekly, monthly, or term-long bus passes; and some charge all students a "bus fee" each term. This is simply a surcharge slapped onto every student's bill.

Solution 1: Get your money's worth and try riding the bus. You may find it more convenient than you thought—and you can study while you travel.

Solution 2: Get a group of your friends together and take a bus cruise once per term. For maximum silliness and fun, dress as formally as you can; white gloves and top hats are ideal. Arrange with your friends to meet at a designated stop and time. As you get in, tip your hat to the driver and say something like "Once around campus, please, James." Sit with your friends and let the bus take you on a pleasure cruise around campus. If you like, point out important landmarks such as cafeteria dumpsters and birdshit-spattered statues. Get off the bus where you got on, and tell yourself that you managed to get at least *something* out of your bus fee.

Bus cruises work best in the late evening and early morning, when campus buses are nearly empty.

6

Advisors

Advisors often give bad advice.

There are two types of advisors:

(1) Regular college teachers. At most liberal arts colleges and a few other schools, each instructor serves as a part-time advisor to a small group of students. These advisors range from very helpful to somewhat harmful.

(2) Full-time advisors whose sole job is to advise students on their academic programs. Community colleges, large universities, business colleges, and technical and vocational schools usually have a few to a few dozen full-time advisors on staff. At technical, vocational, and business colleges, these advisors run the whole range from excellent to awful. At community colleges and large universities, however, advisors are almost invariably narrow-minded, misinformed, over-worked, and educationally dangerous. With astonishing frequency, their advice will hurt you rather than help you.

Solution: Take everything your advisor says with an enormous quantity of skepticism. Consider it carefully; check its accuracy by reading your college's catalog and/or calling the appropriate dean or department office; then make your own decision.

Few students are aware of this simple fact: You don't have to do what your advisor suggests or even insists that you do. *Your advisor cannot force you to do anything. You are the one who plans your overall program and decides each term what to register for, not your advisor.*

If the advice an advisor gives you seems silly, irrelevant, inappropriate, or not in your best interest, disregard it. Don't bother to argue; just thank the advisor, leave his office, and do what you believe is best.

Here's something else most students don't realize: You do not have to passively accept whatever advisor is assigned to you. *You can almost always change your advisor whenever you like.* Usually all it takes is getting your new advisor's signature on a form. Call your registration office for instructions on making this change.

If you attend a college where teachers double as advisors, your advisor should be a teacher whom you like and respect—ideally but not necessarily someone in a department in which you plan to take several courses. (At some colleges, your advisor must be someone who teaches in the department in which you plan to major.) Chapter 7 describes in detail how to locate the best instructors.

If your school has a staff of full-time advisors, finding a decent advisor will be much tougher, and perhaps impossible. Ask for recommendations from teachers and other students you trust, and/or make appointments with a couple of different advisors and ask them about their educational philosophies. An advisor who seems to genuinely want to help you, and who appears generally friendly and knowledgeable, is probably worth trying. However, any advisor who doesn't seem to care about you and your goals is best avoided. Also avoid advisors who have vague or platitude-ridden educational philosophies (or no educational philosophies at all).

Whomever you end up with as an advisor, don't rely upon him too much. Plan to make your own decisions; trust and believe in yourself.

Many advisors will not fully understand your college's rules, regulations, and graduation requirements, even though they may think and insist that they do.

This problem is caused in part by the complexity and profusion of college rules, and the fact that they are frequently changed. It is also caused in part by advisors' laziness, ignorance, and inability to grasp fine points or note exceptions.

Solution: Whenever an advisor informs you of a regulation or tells you that you must do something because the rules require it, write down what she says. Later, after you have left her office, check the information she gave you against the most recent edition of your college's catalog. If the catalog and your advisor agree, assume that what your advisor said is accurate. But if the catalog says otherwise, or it if says nothing about the subject at all, call the office of the appropriate dean or department to find out what the regulation *really* says. To be sure you understand the regulation fully, *ask if there are any exceptions or additional details.* Often there will be some, and sometimes they will directly affect you.

If what the person in the department or dean's office says contradicts what your advisor told you, believe this person, not your advisor.

Your advisor may not be aware of all the educational options available to you.

Advisors do not always keep up with all the changes and additions in regulations, programs, and educational offerings. This is true at colleges of all types, but especially at liberal arts schools.

Solution: Each year, when your college's new catalog comes out, read it very carefully, and make note of any programs, options, and opportunities that interest you. For more information on any of these opportunities, do *not* consult your advisor; directly contact the person or office that coordinates that opportunity.

Also pay attention to posters, announcements in your mailbox, and items in your college newspaper. If something looks potentially interesting, write yourself a note to check into it later.

Most advisors will urge you to take more courses or credits than you can reasonably handle. They may also suggest that you take several difficult classes at once.

These are two of the biggest sins that advisors commit, and they commit them woefully often. At some large universities, advisors often encourage students to take eighteen or twenty credits per term, which translates to 60–70 hours per week of classes and study (90–110 hours per week toward the end of the term).

Solution: As I explained in chapter 3, most colleges expect full-time students to handle a huge workload. Limit yourself to three or four full courses per term, *no matter what your advisor suggests.* And if you work full-time, one course per term is plenty, and two the absolute maximum. It's easy for an advisor to glibly urge you to take on too much—after all, he's not the one who will have to stay up all night studying.

Be especially wary of suggestions that you fill up your schedule with labor-intensive academic courses (English, psychology, chemistry, economics, etc.). Such a schedule will make enormous demands of your time, energy, and patience.

To both survive and enjoy college, you need to balance out the difficult courses with some that are easier or more fun. Regardless of what your advisor says or believes, it is *not* in your best interest to drive yourself crazy by taking nothing but academic classes. For the sake of your happiness and sanity, take at least one fun class—in drawing, dance, yoga, creative writing, photography, electronic music, etc.—each term.

Most advisors—unwisely—urge freshmen to get all their introductory and required courses out of the way during their first two years. The result is often two years of misery.

This is like advising you to eat all your meals for the week on Monday so that you can get them over with.

The theory behind this terrible advice is that once you finish all of your required courses—typically in two years of full-time study—you can then move on to the courses you really want to take. But think about it for a moment. The result is that you spend your entire freshman and sophomore years taking classes you don't want to take. Is this any way to spend two years of your life?

Solution: Ignore any advice to buckle down, grit your teeth, and finish all your requirements as quickly as possible. Do precisely the opposite: Deliberately spread out the required but unappealing courses over your entire college career, so that you are able to take at least some enjoyable classes each term.

Your advisor may implore you to reconsider or tell you that you are making a big mistake. Or she may say, with her voice full of doom, "Now you'll wind up still fulfilling requirements in your junior year," as if this were a fate worse than death. But what in the world is wrong with spreading out your requirements so that you can enjoy your life and at least some of your courses?

Furthermore, you may be able to get out of some (perhaps even all) of the standard required courses—by getting a sufficiently high score on a placement or exemption exam, by completing a similar course at another institution, by studying the subject on your own, by doing an internship, and/or by demonstrating that you have the equivalent knowledge or experience. See pages 121 and 122 for details. You may also be able to avoid certain requirements by designing your own major and/or academic program; for more information, see page 156.

Some advisors will encourage you to study (or even major in) a subject or field that interests them, regardless of whether or not it interests you.

Some advisors try to make their advisees into clones of themselves. Others cling to cherished ideas and try to mold students to fit those ideas, regardless of what those students may actually want or need. Still others simply cannot fathom that what fascinates them might not fascinate all their advisees.

Solution: As before, ignore any advice that doesn't serve your own educational goals and needs. Make your own best choices, knowing that your advisor may strongly disagree. If necessary, look for a new advisor.

Be particularly wary of sweeping generalities such as "Every student should be exposed to the study of botany" or "You can't really claim to be well educated unless you've studied Plato." All such generalities have the same translation: "I have an idea about what higher education is or should be, and I want you to conform to that idea."

Many advisors will not consider who you are as a human being. They will simply steer you toward a preprogrammed course sequence based on your major or stated interests.

Ideally, an advisor should take the time to find out who you are and where your interests lie, then recommend a hand-tailored group of courses and other educational activities that will most help you to learn and grow.

In practice, advisors are more likely to say something like this: "So you're interested in South American history, are you? Here's a list of the course requirements for majoring in history. Give me a call if you have any questions."

Solution 1: If you want good advice on choosing courses, other instructional activities, or a major, don't go to your advisor. Go to an instructor whom you trust; ask your fellow students; and ask department secretaries, all of whom know a great deal about every course and instructor in their departments.

Solution 2: If the preplanned course sequence for a major or minor doesn't suit you very well, or if your college does not offer a major in the field that most interests you, you may be able to design your own major. These majors are usually called individual majors, individualized majors, joint majors, or interdisciplinary majors. These majors allow you to pursue your interests in a unified way without your having to conform to a standard and less-than-appropriate course sequence. Most colleges offer some variation of this option; contact the office of your dean for details.

At some schools it is possible to design your own complete academic program, which is not subject to the normal rules and requirements. This option is described and discussed on page 156.

Some third-rate colleges instruct their advisors to steer students into certain programs regardless of their interests, simply to increase enrollments in those programs.

One student I know was interested in engineering. When he told an advisor about this interest, the advisor replied, "I think you should go into our agriculture program." The student, taken aback, responded, "I'm not interested in agriculture. In fact, I hate agriculture. I want to become an engineer." The advisor answered, "I still think you should try out our agriculture program. How do you know you won't like it if you haven't tried it?"

Solution: If something like this happens to you, dump your advisor immediately. He hasn't got your interests at heart at all—in fact, he doesn't give a damn about you. Find a new advisor—and in the meantime, sign up for whatever courses and/or major you please.

If a second advisor gives you the same line, both are probably following a sleazy directive from above. Ignore them both. You may also be better off transferring to another college; the one you're enrolled in now clearly doesn't care one smidgen about you or your needs.

If you are thinking of dropping a course because you are having serious trouble in it or have fallen two or more weeks behind, your advisor will almost certainly urge you to stick with it and try to catch up. However, ninety-five percent of the time, this is the worst possible advice.

Most advisors and teachers react with a knee-jerk "stick it out" whenever a student asks them about dropping a course. But once you are far enough behind in a class, or sufficiently confused or lost, catching up again is a slim possibility at best.

Solution: You are usually much better off cutting your losses by dropping the class (or auditing it) and focusing your efforts elsewhere. Remember, you can almost always take the class again later.

If your advisor urges you to stay in the class and try to catch up, ignore her. In fact, under the above circumstances you are probably better off not asking her advice at all.

7

Teachers

College teachers range from exciting and inspiring to utterly incompetent.
This is true of people in all professions, not only college instructors. But incompetent college instructors often manage to keep their jobs, get tenure, and even become heads of their departments.

Incompetence in teaching takes many forms. Some teachers are poor lecturers, some poor listeners, and some poor thinkers. Some are disorganized, some pompous, and some just plain boring. Some simply don't give a damn about the people or material they teach.

Incompetence is hardly the rule, however. About half of all college teachers do a decent to excellent job of teaching. Compare this to most high schools, where only one in three teachers does a competent job.

Competence and incompetence are evenly distributed among teachers of all ages, reputations, and academic ranks. The single worst teacher I ever had in college was a highly respected and nationally known full professor who was also the head of his department. Some of the best teachers I have ever seen have been lowly teaching assistants. (Incidentally, despite their title, may teaching assistants don't assist anyone, but teach their own classes.)

What you want in an instructor is someone who knows his or her subject well; who can speak, think, and listen well; who cares about you and about your education; who is willing and available to help you; and who is at least moderately interesting in class.

A good instructor can make almost any subject interesting—even one you've never cared about before. A bad one can make even the most fascinating subject dull. This means it's important to choose your instructors at least as carefully as you do your classes.

Solution: Do not leave the selection of your teachers to chance. *You have the right—and the power—to take courses only from those instructors you find most capable, helpful, and interesting.*

Far too many students let themselves be taught by second- or third-rate teachers. First they allow themselves to be assigned to classes taught by incompetents, fools, or petty tyrants; then, instead of looking for another class or section, they shrug their shoulders, grit their teeth, and slog through the course, hating every minute of it. Instead of complaining to their teacher or their dean, they complain to each other.

But why put yourself through this agony? Instead, take an active role in selecting your teachers. Follow these steps:

First, ignore things like an instructor's age, sex, academic rank (professor, assistant professor, lecturer, teaching assistant, etc.), experience, publications, or reputation as a scholar. These will tell you absolutely nothing about how well they teach.

When you receive a course schedule for the following term, look through it carefully and make a list of all the classes that most interest you. You may wish to rank these in order of preference. Be sure to note the name of the instructor for each course; if the teacher is named only as "staff," or if no instructor is listed at all, call the appropriate department office to find out the teacher's name.

Once you have a list of instructors for these courses, ask your friends and acquaintances what they know about each of them. Was their course interesting? Were they fair and reasonable? Did they care about their students, and were they willing to help them when necessary? Did they encourage the exchange of ideas, or were they only interested in getting across their own? What were their other strengths and weaknesses?

Students' opinions about some teachers may differ, but you'll find an amazing amount of agreement most of the time. If two students disagree about an instructor, you'll need to make your own judgment—but if two or more say the same thing, assume that they are right on target.

Your primary purpose in getting these opinions is to determine which teachers *not* to take courses from. Drop from your list any teacher who gets two or more "no" votes.

Next, separate the remaining teachers on your list by department. Then visit the appropriate department offices, one at a time. (You can also call, but visiting works better.) Tell the department secretary something like this: "I'm thinking about taking a course in the department next term, but I don't know most of the teachers. Which instructors would you say are the most interesting, the most helpful, and the best to work with?"

Unless she was only recently hired, the department secretary knows every instructor in the department extremely well. She should be able to point you to some of the best people in the department. Take down the name of each person the secretary mentions; also ask for the office hours and location, and office and home phone numbers of each. (Some teachers do not give out their home numbers to students.) Then thank the secretary and say, "I'm thinking about taking ————, which ———— will be teaching. Would you recommend this, or do you think I'd be better off with one of the other instructors you named?"

This is a loaded question, of course. The secretary isn't allowed to say anything like "Avoid Professor George; he's a real schmuck"—but you have given her a chance to hint at it. If she says something like "Professor George is good, too," or "Many students seem to like him," then Professor George is worth considering further. Ask the secretary for his office hours, office location, and home and office phone numbers. But if the secretary says, "I think maybe you'd be better off with ————," she is in fact telling you that Professor George is a rotten choice. Avoid him.

Do *not*, however, avoid the instructors the secretary has recommended, even if initially you were not interested in their courses. Check the course catalog again to see what classes they will be teaching, and think about taking one or more of them.

Now comes the most important part. *If you are unwilling or unable to go through the full teacher-selection process, at least do this part.* Visit each instructor you are considering during his office hours; if you cannot get to his office during this time, call and make an appointment. Once you're there, introduce yourself, explain that you're interested in his course, and ask him to tell you something about it. Find out what the course will cover and what textbooks and other readings it will include. Ask for a copy of the course syllabus; if one hasn't been made up for the following term, ask if one from a previous term is available. Feel free to ask any other pertinent questions you like. Be polite, straightforward, and to the point—and keep your meeting short (under ten minutes) unless you and the teacher get involved in a mutually entertaining conversation.

Part of your purpose is in fact to find out more about the course. But, more important, you are trying to get a feel for the instructor. Is he relaxed or nervous? Clear or confusing? Friendly or distant? Helpful or uninterested? Does he seem concerned with helping you learn—or with enforcing rules? (If the teacher focuses not on what you'll study and learn, but on class rules, on grading, and/or on your own obligations in the course, this is a very bad sign.) Use and trust both your judgment and your gut. If you like the instructor or get a good feeling from him, his class is almost certainly worth taking. If you feel negative or have more than minor misgivings, find a different teacher.

If you are serious about only studying with good teachers, take this process one step further. Take your list of teachers who interest you, and sit in on one of each instructor's current classes. If a teacher is currently offering the same course you are thinking of taking next term, this is obviously your best bet.

Arrange a few minutes before the class begins and ask the teacher if it's okay for you to sit in. If you prefer, make your request in advance, either by phone or when you meet with the teacher in his office. Most teachers will have no problem with your sitting in; some, though, prohibit visitors. (This is their right, and it doesn't mean they're not good teachers.) Sit through the full class, but don't participate unless you are asked or encouraged to. This will give you an excellent feel for what each teacher is like in the classroom.

This little bit of legwork and research will pay off handsomely: It will ensure that you get the best teachers, take the most interesting classes, and get the best possible education. Because you'll be working with good teachers, you're also likely to earn higher grades.

But once you've chosen the best teachers, how can you be sure that you'll be able to get into their classes? Just follow the directions on pages 56–59, where I describe several different strategies that will get you into ninety percent of the classes you want to attend.

Most teachers are not hired for their teaching ability. Some are hired *even though* they are known to be poor teachers.

Most universities, many liberal arts colleges, and some other colleges as well, hire teachers with little or no regard for their teaching ability. Instead, they are hired—and promoted, and granted tenure—almost entirely on the basis of their research, publications, and reputation.

In fact, first-rate instructors with few or no publications are almost certain to be fired after a few years, while mediocre or poor teachers with substantial publications are likely to be granted promotions and tenure. They may even win awards for their teaching (these "teaching" awards are often given out not for teaching at all, but for research and/or publications). I know one college teacher who is almost uniformly disliked and distrusted by his students, and widely regarded as a poor teacher; but he was recently given an Excellence in Teaching award because he had published widely.

All of this is crazy. It is also the norm at many colleges. Fortunately, it is less common at community, junior, technical, vocational, and business colleges than it is at universities and liberal arts colleges.

Solution: Do not trust the choices your college made in hiring its instructors. Decide for yourself which teachers are worth studying with. Follow the advice above.

Furthermore, pay no attention to any award or distinction a teacher may have received—even if she was voted Teacher of the Year. Trust your own judgment first and foremost.

For complete details on the bizarre system of academic hiring, firing, and promoting, see Charles J. Sykes's exposés *ProfScam* (Regnery Gateway, 1988, and St. Martin's Press, 1989) and *The Hollow Men* (Regnery Gateway, 1990). Sykes gets some of his small details wrong, but on the whole he is accurate, perceptive, and insightful.

If you are not careful in selecting your teachers, you could end up being miserable *and* earning low grades.

The less competent or interesting an instructor is, the less interesting and useful the whole course is going to be—and the poorer you are likely to do. Furthermore, the poorest teachers are precisely the ones most likely to be capricious or unfair in their grading. Settling for an incompetent instructor may therefore mean not only tedium and less learning, but lower grades—and perhaps the heartache of being treated unfairly.

Solution: Why expose yourself to this kind of treatment when you don't have to? Use the guidelines above to separate the good instructors from the dorks and the bores.

Choosing your instructors carefully will enable you to avoid most or all of the remaining problems in this chapter. However, the sections that follow will be useful in cases where, despite your best efforts, you find yourself with a teacher who is less than fair, reasonable, or competent.

Some teachers are not very knowledgeable, or are outright ignorant, outside of their own field. Some are not even very knowledgeable in their own field.

Some of the stupidest, most ignorant, and most inarticulate people I have ever met have been college teachers with Ph.D.'s. Of course, many of the brightest, most fascinating, and most knowledgeable people I have ever met have also been college teachers.

Solution: Don't assume someone is wise, or completely informed, or always right just because she's a full professor with tenure or an internationally known expert. Experts make mistakes, too, and sometimes they are biased or misinformed.

Treat your instructors with respect, but don't take what they say as gospel. Listen to what they say carefully, politely, and with a grain of salt. If something one of them says doesn't make sense, ask for clarification—or even challenge it. When you spot a contradiction, say so (politely).

Be still more cautious about information and opinions an instructor gives you on subjects outside of his own field. Just because someone may be a genius in sociology or an authority on Benjamin Franklin doesn't mean he knows what he's talking about when he discusses physics or Islam or the Cubs. Carefully consider what your teachers have to say; then accept what makes sense to you and reject what doesn't.

Some college instructors cannot even speak understandable English.

I am not exaggerating here; indeed, this problem has become so widespread at colleges in the United States that it has become a national scandal.

This problem arises when academic departments hire foreign instructors strictly on the basis of their reputations (or promise) as researchers or scholars—without checking to see if they can speak enough English to give a comprehensible lecture. Often these instructors are graduate students who have come to North America to earn master's degrees or doctorates. Colleges and universities give them teaching assistantships as a means of financial support, but may never test or question their ability to speak English.

Some colleges have made a halfhearted attempt at correcting this problem by requiring all non-English-speaking instructors to take a crash course in English. However, many teachers finish this course still unable to deliver a comprehensible lecture in English.

This is hardly surprising. After all, would you consider yourself qualified to teach in Kenya after studying Swahili for only six weeks? For that matter, can you imagine any organization except a college hiring someone who can't speak decent English for a public-speaking job?

Solution: When you interview a potential teacher and/or sit in on her class, take note of her language skills. If she cannot speak reasonably good English, *do not take her course or section*, no matter how friendly or knowledgeable she may seem. No matter what you do, her class is going to be frustrating, infuriating, and just plain difficult.

If you somehow end up in a course or section where the teacher cannot speak adequate English, drop or transfer out of the class immediately.

College teachers can be vain, pompous, arrogant, vindictive, ditzy, obsessively defensive, childish, selfish, or outright nuts.

They can also be helpful, insightful, warm, caring, inspiring, encouraging, and enlightened. In other words, they're exactly like all other human beings.

Consciously or unconsciously, most people expect college instructors to be more compassionate, altruistic, and emotionally stable than the average cook, computer analyst, or welder. But they aren't. They can be just as friendly and helpful—or just as nasty and petty—as any other group of people.

Here are some of the selfish, egotistical, and vicious things a small minority of college teachers do:

- insult or verbally attack their students, in or out of class

- try to make students feel slow-witted or inferior

- single out students to belittle, harass, or bully

- make racist, sexist, or other bigoted remarks in class

- use foul language or sexual innuendo in class with the clear purpose of offending or upsetting people

- make passes at their students, sometimes in public

Solution: The main reason that some teachers get away with these things is because students let them. Most students, instead of confronting an abusive instructor or complaining about him to their dean, simply allow themselves to be abused. At most they may complain to one another.

However, *if you let yourself take abuse from an unstable instructor, he will only be encouraged to continue abusing you.*

With few exceptions, college teachers are not monitored by deans, other administrators, or even other teachers. In general, then, no administrator knows what goes on in any teacher's class unless a student lets her know. This means that if a teacher mistreats you (or anyone else in your class) and no one confronts him or complains about him, the abuse becomes a kind of secret between the teacher and the class.

If one of your instructors does any of the things listed above—or anything else that you believe is dishonest, disrespectful, intrusive, or abusive—speak to him privately about it *promptly*, either immediately after class or within twenty-four hours. You may do this either in person or by phone, and either alone or with one or more other students from the class. Your complaint will have the most effect if you make it in person with at least one other student.

Begin by explaining firmly and politely to the instructor exactly what he did that you feel is unfair or offensive. *Then, no matter what the teacher says, ask him clearly and firmly not to do it again.*

The teacher may apologize, get angry, deny that what you said is true, tell you that you're imagining things, insist that he was only kidding, start to cry, or even acuse *you* of wrongdoing. Whatever he does, however, simply say again that you want him not to repeat his offensive or unreasonable behavior. Then leave or hang up.

Afterward, write down exactly what your teacher said and did—both what you initially found objectionable and what he did in response to your complaint. Include dates, places, and times.

Much of the time, your complaint will be enough to make the teacher change his ways. If he repeats the offense, however, *do not speak with him about it again.* Simply write down exactly what he did and when and where he did it. Then take your complaint directly and promptly to your dean. Make an appointment in advance, and bring with you your written notes on your teacher's behavior. Again, the more students you can get to accompany you, the greater impact you will have. However, even if you make your complaint alone, the dean will pay very close attention and treat the matter with the seriousness it deserves.

Important: Do not complain to the head of the instructor's department. She may ignore the matter or try to sweep it under the rug, "for the good of the department." Don't deal with anyone with less authority than your dean.

The great majority of deans will do their best to resolve the problem. Indeed, chances are excellent that they have received similar complaints from other students about the instructor before.

Perhaps one dean out of thirty, however, seeking to avoid a scandal, will try to ignore the matter. She may tell you you're making a mountain out of a molehill, or come to the teacher's defense, or—worst of all—try to blame *you* for what happened.

If any of this occurs, leave the dean's office immediately, write down the most complete account of the meeting that you can, and make an appointment with your school's provost. Plan to file formal written complaints about both your teacher and your dean; you may also wish to consider suing the college.

Certain instructors may actually respect you more if you catch and correct their errant behavior. Others, however, may try to punish you for it—most likely with low grades. If you believe that you *are* being punished or graded unfairly, speak with the instructor about it privately. Be polite—but also be firm and assertive. If your discussion with the instructor fails to resolve the problem, see your dean.

Some teachers, consciously or unconsciously, will reward you for agreeing with their ideas and penalize you for disagreeing. Some teachers will even punish you for thinking for yourself or speaking your mind. Some of these closed-minded teachers are widely respected or even famous in their fields.

What's strangest about this is that some of these very same instructors think of themselves as extremely open-minded.

Solution: Be yourself and say what you believe *at first*. Most instructors will appreciate and even reward you for it.

Those instructors who expect you to parrot their own ideas will soon show it—by repeating the same point or principle over and over; by frequently taking, explaining, or defending the same point of view; by returning to the same writer, thinker, or book again and again; or by simply teaching their opinions as facts.

They may also demonstrate their biases negatively, by discounting and criticizing opposing ideas and perspectives, and (especially) by giving poor or mediocre grades to people who support those ideas in papers and/or on tests. Often, but not necessarily, they will write critical comments such as: "Your ideas are not fully formed"; "You haven't really thought your premises through"; "These ideas have already been demonstrated as false"; "Your ideas are simplistic"; or, "You don't actually believe this, do you?"

When you spot one or more of these warning signs, don't try to debate or contradict the instructor's ideas any longer; doing so will only get you into trouble. Instead, focus on ideas, topics, and themes that interest you, *but that do not contradict your instructor's ideas.*

This does not mean you have to pretend to agree with your instructor; just don't disagree with her. For instance, if your teacher is convinced that Marxism is the answer to most social and political problems, don't promote or defend capitalism. But you *could* write a paper about social protest in Iceland, or the Green Party in

Germany—subjects that are neither pro- nor anti-Marxist—and receive a positive response from your teacher. Skirting the potential controversy—instead of uselessly confronting or mindlessly parroting your instructor—gives you the opportunity to earn a high grade and actually learn something, without having to cater to your teacher's biases.

Many teachers live entirely in the tiny, incestuous, self-enclosed world of academia, and haven't the faintest idea what goes on outside of it.

Many college teachers have a very limited frame of reference. They can tell you on what day of the week the Treaty of Utrecht was signed, or the name of Jonathan Swift's maid, but they will have no idea who Oprah Winfrey or Danielle Steel or Bo Jackson is.

Solution: You can't know what is and isn't in a teacher's head. But you *can* do three things:

(1) If you refer to an element of popular culture (e.g., Bart Simpson, Salad Shooters, or "A Current Affair") in a paper or essay test, briefly explain what or who it is, perhaps in parentheses or a footnote.

(2) Don't be surprised if an instructor just doesn't understand a reference or puts a question mark in the margin next to it.

(3) Pity the poor isolated soul.

Some teachers will penalize you if you do not sound scholarly and use the jargon of their field; others will penalize you if you do.

As a college student, you'll be regularly exposed to two kinds of writing: 1) writing that is clear, understandable, and easy to read, and 2) writing that is dull, long-winded, unnecessarily complicated, hard to follow and understand, and peppered with obscure words and specialized terms.

Here's the same idea expressed in these two different languages:

(1) Cats like to chase mice.

(2) It has been repeatedly observed that the majority of *felis cati* show a propensity for pursuing a certain species of *rodentia*. They appear to derive pleasure from this pursuit behavior.

Just so you have no doubts: Sentence number 1 is written well—it's clear, concise, to the point, and easy to understand. Sentence number 2 is awful.

In your composition classes, you will be taught, and expected, to write in language number 1. About half of your other teachers will also expect you to write this way. The other half will expect you to write (and perhaps even speak) in language number 2. These teachers, who are often poor writers and speakers themselves, equate overblown, difficult language with good scholarship. They think, quite wrongly, that clear, straightforward English is too informal or elementary to be used in college writing.

Solution: Write in language number 1—clear, straightforward prose—for every class and every instructor at the beginning of each term. Then see how each instructor responds to your writing. The teachers who value plain English will reward you for using plain English yourself. But a teacher who wants you to use language number 2 will probably give you a mediocre or low grade on your first piece of writing. She may comment on your writing, perhaps by calling it simplistic or too informal; but she is more likely to pretend to criticize your content. Some typical criticisms include "lack of depth," "insufficient understanding of the central concepts [and/or terms]," "surface [or simplistic] understanding," "insufficient serious- ness of purpose," "failure to grapple with the central ideas," "intellectual immaturity," "elementary approach to the topic," and "lack of academic rigor." If you get comments such as these, odds are good that writing in language number 2 next time will get better results. (One exception: If your instructor says that your writing is fine, but your ideas or thinking are not, take what she says at face value.)

Here are some key points to writing in language number 2:

• If a common word can be replaced with a specialized term used widely in that subject, replace it. (For example, instead of "colleges," say "post-secondary educational institutions.")

• Adopt a serious tone and a weighty-sounding style. ("Jones disagrees" thus becomes "Jones asserts a contrary hypothesis.")

• If your instructor uses certain words or phrases regularly in lectures or discussions, use some (not all) of them in your own writing.

• Don't go overboard. Simply modify your style so that it reads more like language number 2 than language number 1.

• Never forget what you're doing or why you're doing it: You're deliberately writing badly for an instructor who prefers bad writing to good. Outside of her class, continue to write as clearly and straightforwardly as you can.

Don't try to explain to your teacher that she is asking you to write badly, or that you were taught different rules for writing in your composition class. You're not likely to change her mind, and she may later get back at you by giving you a low grade. (Instructors who prefer poor writing are not usually paragons of justice.)

Language number 2 is most prevalent in social science fields and in philosophy. It is also fairly common in the study of teaching and education. There are, of course, plenty of social science and philosophy instructors who write very well indeed, and who expect good writing from their students—just as there are teachers in all fields who will expect you to write in language number 2.

Incidentally, the dilemma of being asked to do two precisely opposite things by two different people who have authority over you is not unique to college. It will likely occur a number of times in your future career. Learning how to deal with these contradictory demands is an important skill in working and getting along with others.

Some teachers may "correct" your proper grammar, diction, spelling, punctuation, or even meaning to something that is incorrect or improper.

College teachers, like anyone else, sometimes make mistakes, and sometimes they are simply misinformed about the English language (which is, after all, a difficult and complicated language).

About two-thirds of college teachers in all subjects will critique and correct your writing on papers and tests. Most of the time, they'll know what they're talking about, but sometimes they won't.

One of the most common instances of correcting what's already correct involves the words "a lot," which some teachers improperly correct to "alot." Another example: Many teachers correct "all right" to "alright," while others correct "all right" to "alright." According to most sources, *both* spellings are acceptable.

Solution: If you believe a correction is in fact incorrect, check it against your textbook or the appropriate reference book (the reference librarian in your college library can direct you to the most useful resource). If in fact your teacher is right, you've learned something useful; but if he's wrong, you have two options:

(1) If the instructor seems to be a sane and reasonable person, and doesn't have a huge ego, photocopy the appropriate page of the reference book or textbook. Then meet with him briefly before or after class, or in his office. Show him the correction he made and the photocopied page from the book. Explain politely that to the best of your knowledge, what you originally wrote or said was correct. If you like, you can also say, "Am I missing or misunderstanding something?"

(2) If your teacher seems arrogant, defensive, or egotistical, *don't* correct his correction. Instead, do things his way for the rest of the course. When the course is over, go back to doing things properly again.

When you're having trouble with a course, some teachers may be unwilling or unable to help you.

Some instructors will claim to be (or actually be) too busy. Some will be too lazy or too selfish. Others will try their best to be helpful, but simply may not be able to make something clear to you.

Solution 1: If a teacher has another time commitment or is too busy to give you the help you need right now, make an appointment with her. Explain what you need and how much time you think it will take. Be sure that the teacher schedules at least this much time for you.

If the instructor says, "Why don't you stop by during my office hours?" say yes, but add, "Let's set up an appointment for a specific time during your office hours." If necessary, be assertive and persistent about this; you do not want to have to wait in line during the teacher's office hours, only to be put off again, or be given five hurried, distracted minutes.

If you are not free during the teacher's regular office hours, say so. You have the right to schedule a meeting at some other mutually convenient time.

Solution 2: If your teacher won't or can't offer you the help you need, ask another instructor in the department.

Explain your dilemma to the department secretary, and ask him to recommend two or three teachers who he thinks will be willing to help you. Get the office hours and location, office phone number, and home phone number (if available) for each of these people; then either call to set up an appointment with one of them or stop in during her regular office hours. Explain what you're having trouble with and that your regular teacher has been unable or unwilling to help. Most instructors will take pity on you and do their best to help you.

If you feel your instructor has shirked her duties, feel free to complain about her to your dean.

A great many college instructors don't keep their own office hours.

Some teachers are frequently in and out of their offices during their official hours. Sometimes they post notes that say "back in five minutes" (though they may not return for fifteen or twenty); sometimes they just lock their doors, leaving students to wonder. Others arrive late, sometimes by half an hour or more. Still others often don't show up at all.

Some teachers tell students in advance when they will be unable to keep their office hours; others, however, give no advance notice, and simply leave cryptic notes that say,. "No office hours today; important meeting." Still others will post notes that just say, "Office hours canceled." Yet others will post no notices at all.

Being laissez-faire about office hours is probably college teachers' most frequently committed sin. Even some of the best instructors are guilty of it. I confess to this irresponsibility myself.

Solution 1: Whenever possible, make advance appointments, or speak with instructors before or after class. If you do plan to see a teacher during his office hours, try to make an appointment: If you just show up, you may find yourself in line behind four or five other students. Not only will you have to wait, but by the time your turn arrives the teacher's office hours may be over—and he may have to leave for a commitment elsewhere.

Solution 2: If your situation can be adequately dealt with by phone, call the instructor, either in his office or at home (if he has given you his home phone number).

Many teachers are in their offices at times other than their official office hours. If your teacher is busy when you call, set up a specific time when the two of you will talk by phone.

If you call a teacher during his regular office hours and get no answer, try again ten minutes later—and, if necessary, ten minutes after that.

Many teachers will regularly be late for appointments. Some will regularly cancel and reschedule—or cancel and not reschedule—appointments.

Some teachers are just too busy, some lazy, some thoughtless, some poor at managing their time, and some all four.

Solution: Whenever possible, give teachers until twenty minutes after your scheduled meeting time to show up (or to finish their previous meeting). Always bring with you something to read or do so you won't have to twiddle your thumbs as your wait.

If after twenty minutes the teacher hasn't arrived, leave a note on her door with this message: "Dear ———: We had an appointment for ———. I waited until ——— for you. Please call me at ——— as soon as possible to reschedule. I have several questions regarding ——— for you [or, I need your help with ———, etc.]." If the instructor does not call you within two days, call her yourself.

If your instructor is meeting with another student when you arrive, wait for ten minutes. If the meeting still isn't over, knock on the door and say politely, "Just letting you know that I'm here." If, after half an hour, the previous appointment still hasn't ended, knock again; if you like, suggest that your appointment be rescheduled.

If a teacher cancels an appointment, reschedule it on the spot, or as soon thereafter as possible. If a phone appointment will work just as well, offer this option.

Some instructors are always busy or in a rush. These teachers may treat you curtly, try to get rid of you quickly, or never have time for you at all.

In some cases, your teacher may simply be a nervous, fast-paced person. Most likely, however, he is overcommitted, overworked, and unable to adequately manage his time.

Nevertheless, as an instructor he has an obligation to help you and, if necessary, to work one-on-one with you.

Solution: Don't let a teacher's busyness or nervousness rub off on you. Calmly and politely ask for and claim the help you need.

If an instructor appears to be pressed for time, ask if he would prefer to schedule a future appointment (or, if appropriate, a telephone conversation) at a mutually convenient time.

It is also an excellent idea to announce at the beginning of any meeting or phone call exactly what it is you need and about how long you expect the call or meeting to take. If your instructor cannot spare this amount of time, do as much as you can now, then set up a later appointment or call to finish the discussion.

Meanwhile, do your best to stick to your agenda and complete as much of it as possible. If the conversation wanders, bring it back to the matter at hand.

If a teacher tries to hurry you through a meeting, looks at his watch frequently, or even sighs or grimaces at your questions, do not be intimidated. Simply ask, "How much more time can you afford to give me now? Would you rather we set up an appointment to meet or talk on the phone later?" Then spend whatever remaining time you now have, if any, dealing with the issues that concern you—at whatever pace you need.

If you are doing badly in a class, and ask your instructor whether you should stay in it or drop it, she will almost invariably urge you to stick with it, no matter how far behind you are, no matter how little of the material you understand, and no matter what other obligations or responsibilities you may have. Nevertheless, if you end up doing badly in the course, the instructor will insist that the decision to stay in it was entirely your own, and that you are solely to blame for your low grade.

Solution: Don't ask for your instructor's advice. You know your circumstances better than she does. Make the decision on your own.

If you're having a great deal of difficulty with a course, sometimes the very best thing to do is drop it—then take it again in a later term. On your second try, you'll have a much better chance of doing well, because you'll already have some instruction in the subject under your belt.

Another option is to change your status in the course to that of an auditor. An auditor is someone who takes a course for no credit and no grade. This enables you to continue to attend the course, receive help from the instructor, and learn about the subject without the danger of earning a low grade. Usually you may do as much or as little of the work as you please, though some instructors may insist on a minimum level of participation. You can become an auditor in any of your classes by filling out a simple form; call your registration office for details. (Important: Be sure you make the official change *only for the individual class you wish to audit*, not for all of your courses.)

The best time to decide whether to stick with a course, audit it, or drop it is a few days before the deadline to drop classes. At some schools this deadline comes as late as just before final exams; at some others, it is as early as the second week of the term. Typically, the deadline is about halfway through the term. This deadline should be noted in the course schedule; if it is not, check with your registration office.

As this deadline nears, look carefully at any course that you are having real trouble in—that is, any course where you are doing less than "C" (or average) work. Consider how much difficulty you are having, how confused or far behind you are, how much time you will need to catch up, how much time you will be able to devote to the class in the future, and how well you believe you will be able to do in the remainder of the course. If the prospects look reasonably positive, stick with the course; if they look pretty grim, bail out or become an auditor while you can. Remember, you can almost certainly take the class again later, possibly even with the same instructor. (Note: The deadline to switch your registration to an audit is usually—but not necessarily—the same as the deadline for dropping classes. Contact your registration office for details.)

Do keep in mind that dropping below a certain number of courses or credits per term may affect your financial aid status. Contact your financial aid office for details. At some of the most high-powered colleges, you may also need to complete a minimum number of courses or credits per term to remain in good academic standing; check your college catalog or call your registration office for detailed information.

The instructor who teaches a course may not be the person who grades your papers, tests, and/or exams.

In many courses (particularly introductory courses) at most universities, full-time instructors do most or all of the lecturing. A teaching assistant, however, may be responsible for grading your assignments and tests. TAs may also be responsible for supervising labs and/or leading small-group discussions. (At all schools *except* universities, however, the instructor of a class almost always does his own grading.)

There is one other situation in which one person may do the teaching and another the grading. This is when two or more regular faculty members team-teach a class, and only one of them does the grading. This arrangement can occur at a college of any type.

Solution: If you are unhappy with a grade you've been given, speak first to the person who read and graded your work; follow the advice on pages 148–150. If this doesn't resolve the matter, then take your case to the other instructor. (If you're not sure who graded your work, of course ask.)

If you have a regular instructor and a TA, and you like the regular instructor but are unhappy with your TA, ask the regular instructor to switch you to a different discussion section (or lab, etc.) run by another TA. Explain quite straightforwardly that you're not happy with the TA you've been assigned to, and feel free to say why.

The person listed as the instructor of a class in the course schedule may not be the person who actually teaches the class. You may even have instructors switched on you as late as the first week of the term.

This is rarely a deliberate bait-and-switch. Any of the following scenarios is possible:

• The instructor who had originally agreed to teach the course resigned, retired, died, or took a leave of absence.

• Two or more instructors agreed (with department approval) to teach each other's courses.

• The department made a decision to reassign the course to a different instructor. This happens most frequently with introductory courses taught by teaching assistants.

Sometimes the instructor of a course will be listed in the course schedule as "staff." This simply means that when the class schedule went to press, an instructor for the course had not yet been found or determined.

Solution: Interview the new instructor according to the advice on pages 95–96. If you don't like what she does and says, or if you're unhappy with the first one or two class meetings, consider transferring to a different course or section.

If you plan to study with a particular teacher—or if you enroll in a particular college in order to study under him—he may no longer be teaching there when the next term begins.

College instructors are notorious for disappearing from campus for a year or two. They are equally notorious for moving from one school to another every few years. An instructor might, for example:

• Go on sabbatical (paid leave) for a term or a year to travel, write, or do research. Most teachers earn a sabbatical every five to ten years.

• Take an unpaid leave of absence to travel, write, do research, or complete a doctorate.

• Serve as a visiting instructor for a year or two at another college.

Instructors also leave teaching to take administrative jobs as department heads, deans, and so on. And of course some instructors quit, retire, or die.

Solution: If you wish to study with a certain instructor, call him during his office hours and ask if he will be teaching on campus during the following term or year. While you're at it, ask what courses he will be teaching and what entrance requirements and/or prerequisites, if any, there will be for each course.

If the teacher is not on campus during the current term, call his department secretary for this information.

Some faculty members don't teach undergraduate classes. Some don't teach any classes at all.

Some universities and liberal arts colleges hire "research professors": people whose sole job is to do research and/or scholarship. Sometimes they work entirely on their own; sometimes they are assisted by graduate students and/or advanced undergraduates. They teach no classes. (They *may* sponsor a few independent study projects each term, but usually only for the top students in their departments.)

Many universities vary this theme a bit by hiring "teachers" who in fact teach only one class per term—or only graduate classes, or only one or two undergraduate classes each year.

Solution: Same as above. Make sure you find out exactly who may enroll in each class, and what prerequisites and/or entrance requirements there are, if any, for each.

No matter how much you may want to study with a certain teacher, you may simply not be permitted to, even if she teaches undergraduate classes.

Some big-name instructors teach only honors and/or graduate courses. Others may require students to submit a sample of their work, and will work with only those students they believe are most talented. Still others may teach courses that are open only to seniors, or juniors and seniors.

Solution: Same as above. If a work sample is required, submit the very best one you can.

When you ask instructors for recommendations, some may insist that you waive your right to see what they write about you.

When you apply for jobs, merit scholarships and fellowships, or admission to graduate or professional school, you will usually be asked for recommendations from some of your college teachers. Furthermore, when you set up a placement file in your college's career placement office during your final year of college, you will want to include recommendations from instructors.

You have the right to see any and all recommendations that any teacher writes for you—unless that teacher specifically asks you to waive your right of access to what he writes. However, many instructors—perhaps half—*will* ask you to waive this right. Some may even refuse to write a recommendation if you do not waive your right. (Some instructors routinely ask all students to waive their right of access, as a matter of policy.)

An instructor may have either of these two reasons for asking you to waive this right:

(1) Agreeing not to see what someone writes about you means, at least theoretically, that he is able to be completely honest when evaluating you. Recommendations which you do not get to see there-

fore carry a little more weight than those which you are permitted to look at. (I always ask recommendees to officially waive their right of access for this reason; then I send them copies of my recommendations anyway.)

(2) The instructor does not want you to see what he writes about you because it is lukewarm, equivocal, or downright critical of you.

Solution: In general, agree to waive your right of access if you are asked to, without argument. In fact, if a recommendation form has a place for you to waive your right of access, do so routinely, even if you are not asked to.

However, pick the instructors you ask recommendations from quite carefully. You want to make sure that what gets written about you is as favorable as possible. Ask for recommendations *only* from those instructors who know your work reasonably well, who have been at least somewhat impressed with it, and who seem both fair and friendly. Do not ask for a recommendation from anyone who has not given you at least a B. You do not want to end up with a halfhearted recommendation—or, worse, a "recommendation" that expresses doubts and misgivings.

If any instructor turns down your request for a recommendation, or even expresses more than minor reluctance ("Can't you get one from another teacher?," "I'm not sure if I'm the right person to write this," etc.), do *not* press the issue. Let him off the hook, because anything he might write for you will be unenthusiastic at best.

Some teachers will need to be reminded that they owe you recommendations. Some will need to be reminded repeatedly.

About half of all teachers are very good at writing and sending in recommendations on time. About half need to be monitored and, when necessary, politely badgered into compliance.

Solution: Make your request for a recommendation four to five weeks before it is due—or, if this is impossible, as soon as you can. Let your instructor know exactly when the recommendation *must be received* (not mailed). If a special recommendation form must be used, get it to her immediately.

Ten days before the deadline, call the instructor and ask if she has mailed the recommendation. If she says no, remind her of the impending deadline, and ask her to be sure she meets or beats it.

Check again three or four days before the deadline. If she still has not sent in your recommendation, explain politely but urgently that the deadline for receiving it has almost arrived. At this point it is a good idea to ask her to send it via overnight delivery; volunteer to reimburse her for the cost. (Few teachers will actually ask you for the money.)

Make a final call on the day of the deadline; if necessary, have your teacher fax her recommendation.

Ninety-five percent of all teachers will, with reminders and coaxing, get recommendations in on time. If one of your instructors doesn't, you should of course never ask her for another recommendation.

8

Administrators and Staff

If you have a problem, particularly one caused by a computer error, some staff people will automatically assume and/or act as if the fault is entirely yours.

I've overheard support people (secretaries, data entry clerks, etc.) tell students countless times, "Well, if you had only _____ instead of _____, this wouldn't have happened." But putting the blame on you doesn't do a thing to solve the problem; all it does is make you feel defensive or guilty.

Solution: It is the job of support people to help you, regardless of who is to blame for your problem. Even if the situation *is* your fault, they are still responsible for helping you to set things right.

So don't let people sidetrack you with the issue of who is to blame. Resist the urge to defend yourself, and instead simply say, "I'm sorry that it happened, and I plan to do everything I can to make sure it doesn't happen again. But right now I need your assistance. Will you help me, please?" Be firm without being nasty or aggressive.

This strategy will work ninety percent of the time. But if it doesn't, go to the staff person's superior. Explain the situation and ask him to help you instead.

Some staff people and administrators may promise to help you, then do nothing.

Usually this is an oversight or an honest mistake, not an act of laziness, a lack of consideration, or hostility. But once in a great while

116

you may encounter someone who deals with requests by making promises and then doing nothing.

Solution: Always follow up on any action an administrator or staff member agrees to perform on your behalf, whether it's sending out a transcript or fixing a billing error or transferring in credits from another school. Give that person a reasonable amount of time to fix the problem or fulfill your request. If, within that time, you don't receive confirmation that she has done what you asked her to, speak to her again. Repeat your request—straightforwardly, firmly, and perhaps a bit urgently. But don't plead or get angry. Once again give the person a reasonable length of time to do what she promised to do—and check on her if she does not confirm that she has fulfilled your request.

If by this time she still has failed to help you, take the matter out of her hands. *Do not give her a third chance; you will almost surely be wasting your time.* Take your request to someone else.

That "someone else" should generally be that person's superior. However, if someone else in the office has the identical job, authority, and access to information, you may also go to him. Explain exactly what has happened so far—and what has failed to happen—and ask for his assistance.

With few exceptions, this should set things straight for you. But if for some reason it doesn't, go to *that* person's superior.

If you have a problem, the suggestion the administrator or staff person gives you for solving it may not work.

As I explained in chapter 4, many college employees may not fully understand all of the school's policies and regulations, even though they may think and say that they do. Although they will usually give you their best advice, sometimes that advice may simply be wrong.

Solution: Whenever you are given any directions or information by a college employee, check it on the spot by repeating it and asking him if you've heard it correctly. Example: "Let me make sure I understand. I need to take this form to the head of the chemistry department, get her secretary's signature, and then return it to you. Is that right?" Also be sure to get the name of the person who gives you the information; you might say, for example, "Can you give me your name, in case I have any questions about this later?"

If this person's information turns out to be wrong, or if his suggestion fails to work, call or visit him again. Try to speak with the same person, not just anyone in the same office. If he is not in, find out when he will be.

Once you get hold of him, give your name and explain what happened. Say once more what the problem is and what you want to have happen. Repeat what you believe he told you to do, explain exactly what steps you took, and tell him what the final result was. Then say, "Something still isn't working. Can you help me to straighten it out?" Be polite but firm; don't panic, whine, grovel, or act nasty.

Usually this person will immediately get on the phone and attempt to solve your problem for you—or give you new information that will enable you to solve it yourself. But if, for some reason, he is unwilling or unable to help you, go to his superior.

One other tip: If, when someone gives you information or instructions, he seems uncertain, say to him, "You seem a little unsure. Are you certain that's how it works, or would you like to check to make sure?" If the person *is* unsure, this encourages him to find out the correct information and pass it on to you.

Some staff people will be rude to you and/or treat you like a child.
You'll run into such people occasionally throughout your life—not just at colleges, but at restaurants, stores, and government offices as well. Try one or more of the following strategies with such a person:

Solution 1: Ignore their attitude, and firmly but politely stick to the business at hand.

Solution 2: Politely confront her anger with a question like this: "Did I do something to make you angry? I'm sorry if I did; I wasn't trying to."

Solution 3: Show her a little empathy. Smile and say, "It sounds like some other people have been giving you a hard time about this." Usually this will soften her up; but if she responds with, "Why?" just say, "Oh, you seemed a little upset a moment ago."

Solution 4: If none of the above works, deal with another person—either someone else with the same title and responsibilities, or a superior. If necessary, let the superior know how the first person treated you.

If you have a nonstandard question, request, problem, or situation, some administrators and staff people will not understand—or even hear—what you say to them.

Ninety-eight percent of all the situations these people deal with are standard and routine. After a while, they start *expecting* everything to be routine. Eventually they stop listening to other people carefully; they just pay attention to key words and give a different automatic response to each key word.

For instance, if you ask the secretary in the financial aid office to send you a photocopy of the completed financial aid form you filed two years ago, all she might hear is, "Send me a financial aid form"— and she'll send you a blank one for the following year.

Solution: If your request, question, or situation seems at all unusual, plan to explain yourself very carefully—more than once, if necessary.

Begin your explanation or request with, "I have a rather unusual problem" or "I need your help with an unusual situation." Explain your circumstances in detail. When you are done, say once again what makes your situation unusual or special.

If the person you are dealing with seems to respond in an automatic, preprogrammed way, check one more time. Say, "And this applies even in cases like mine?" If he says yes, believe him. If he hesitates or isn't sure, ask, "Would you check it for me to make sure?"

This strategy will work with all but the most dimwitted administrators and staff people. If it *doesn't* work with someone, avoid him like the plague for the rest of your college career.

9

Classes and Other Forms of Learning

If you take a class without carefully considering who teaches it, what emphasis it has, and what readings, assignments, and tests it will include, you could be stuck with a class you hate—*and* a low grade.

College courses range from the fascinating to the mediocre to the intolerable. Why take mediocre or intolerable classes when you don't have to? A little careful shopping can make a world of difference.

Solution: You already know from chapter 7 how essential it is to choose your teachers carefully. In that chapter I explained exactly how to locate the best instructors; now here's how to shop for the best courses taught by these instructors.

First, when you interview an instructor, ask for a copy of the appropriate course syllabus. Read it carefully; if you need more information, ask for it.

Take a look at the required reading as soon as you can. You should be able to locate most or all of the books in your college bookstore and/or library. If any of the books looks impossibly technical, difficult, unreadable, or dull, avoid taking that class. If the class is required, scan the textbooks for other sections to see if any of those texts are any better.

Be aware that the required reading for the same course taught by the same instructor can sometimes vary a bit (or more than a bit) from term to term.

If, after making your best and most informed choice, you realize during the first week or two of the term that the course will be awful or impossibly difficult, drop it.

Different sections of the same course can be enormously different.
In general, when two or more sections of the same course are offered, each instructor is free to run his own section however he pleases. Thus, different sections may have different formats, syllabi, required books, or criteria for grading. They may even differ in their overall content and approach. As a result, it is quite possible for one section of a course to be fascinating, and another painfully dull.

Solution: Assume that different sections of the same course will differ greatly. Use the tips above and in chapter 7 to pick the instructor and section that are best for you.

Some prerequisites or course sequences are unnecessary or irrelevant.
Many intermediate and advanced classes have prerequisites—courses that normally must be completed first. Some departments and majors also have preplanned sequences of three or more courses which students are urged or required to complete.

Most of the time, these prerequisites and sequences make sense; but sometimes they are inappropriate or unnecessary.

Solution 1: If you wish to take a course but have not completed the prerequisite, you can get the prerequisite waived if you can demonstrate to the instructor that you have the skills or knowledge necessary to understand the material and complete the course. Some ways of demonstrating this include:

• getting a sufficiently high score on an advanced placement exam, Achievement Test, College-Level Examination Program test, department placement or exemption exam, or other test

• completing a credit *or noncredit* course similar to the prerequisite at another institution—preferably but not necessarily another college or university

• extensively studying the subject the prerequisite covers on your own, either informally or in an official independent study

- gaining direct experience in the prerequisite's subject via a job, an internship, fieldwork, etc.

Meet with the instructor before the term begins—or, if necessary, during the first week of the term. Present your evidence that you are ready and able to handle the material in her class, and ask to have the prerequisite waived. If your evidence is reasonable, most instructors will grant your request.

If for some reason the instructor says no, you can of course try the same strategy with another instructor who teaches a different section of the same course.

Solution 2: With very few exceptions, registration computers do not check to see if students have the necessary prerequisites to take the courses they register for; nor do they check to see if students are taking courses in the recommended sequence. If you believe you can do well in a course even though you lack the official prerequisite or are taking it out of sequence, just sign up for it without asking anyone's permission. Chances are no one will check on you—or, for that matter, care whether or not you are following the rules.

If, for some reason, an instructor does check whether or not students have completed the appropriate prerequisite, use solution 1 above.

Incidentally, many course sequences are recommendations only, not requirements. Your college catalog and/or the appropriate department handbook will tell you which courses absolutely must be taken in sequence.

The number of credits awarded for a class may have little or nothing to do with the actual amount of work required for that class.
Instructors differ widely in what they believe is an appropriate amount of work to require for a course.

Solution: Make no assumptions about the amount of work a class requires based on the number of credits you will receive for it. Instead, get specific answers. Talk to the instructor, read the syllabus, and look at the required reading.

Most introductory courses require a great deal of work.
Don't let the words "introduction to," "introductory," or "beginning" mislead you. Introductory courses in academic subjects (history,

chemistry, English, psychology, etc.) are often among the most labor-intensive courses that colleges offer. Because they give you a broad background on an entire field, these courses usually require lots of reading and studying; some require lab work as well.

Solution: Avoid taking more than two introductory courses in academic subjects per term. If this isn't possible—and it may not be during your first term or two—take the most interesting courses you possibly can.

Many college classes are boring. Many involve little or nothing more than memorizing and regurgitating information from textbooks and lectures.

None of this surprises you, I'm sure. Most of your high school classes were probably the same.

Solution: Just because most classes are dull does not mean that *you* have to take any of the dull ones. In fact, refuse to take them. College is not like high school; in college you have the power to make choices.

Use the tips in chapter 7 and earlier in this chapter to find the best instructors and classes. When you find good teachers, stick with them; when a class you've chosen turns out to be a dud in the first week or two, drop it and replace it with something better.

What you are taught in one class may contradict what you are taught in another.

Sometimes this is the result of a legitimate difference in opinion or perspective. At other times, however, one person may simply be right and the other wrong.

Solution: Photocopy or write down the pieces of contradicting information. Then visit one (or, if you like, both) of the appropriate instructors in their offices. Explain that you're confused about something, that you've heard a couple of different ideas on the subject, and that you'd like their help in resolving some apparent contradictions. Show them the conflicting pieces of information; then let them talk.

It is essential that you be polite, tactful, and friendly when you do this. Present yourself as someone seeking insight and clarification (which you are), *not* as a smartass trying to catch your instructor in an error.

This process will not always resolve the contradiction, but it will at least give you more insight into both people's perspectives and a better grasp of the key concepts and problems involved.

This procedure also works well if the same teacher has given you what appear to be two or more contradictory pieces of information.

Teachers often do not follow their own syllabi.

Instructors are not required to follow their syllabi to the letter. In fact, many instructors use a syllabus simply as a rough outline which they amend as needed as the course proceeds.

This can become a problem is you miss a class and use the information on the syllabus to prepare for the next meeting. You may show up well prepared for a discussion that has been postponed for a week, yet unprepared for what goes on in class.

Solution: Don't take any syllabus as gospel. If you miss a class meeting, call either the instructor or another student in the course as soon as possible to find out what you missed, what will take place next time, and what reading, writing, and other assignments will be due then.

During the first meeting of any class, be sure to get and write down your instructor's office phone number, office hours, and, if she is willing to give it out, her home phone number. During the first two weeks of the term, also find another student in the class to exchange phone numbers with; make a deal with him that one of you can call the other for information if you miss a class. It is important that you get the phone number of at least one student, because instructors are sometimes difficult to contact.

If you are a late riser, signing up for an early morning class (or even a late morning class) is usually a mistake.

People who are used to sleeping in have a terrible time getting to morning classes on time, or at all. Many are perennially late; others are perennially absent; some end up dropping or flunking the class. A few do all right at the beginning of the fall term, but as the sun rises later and the weather gets colder, they find it harder and harder to get out of bed in the early morning.

Some late risers take morning classes in the hope that this will somehow force them to change their habits and get up earlier. This tactic almost never works; even if they do manage to get to class, they are usually too sleepy to pay much attention or participate fully. Sometimes they doze off right in class.

Solution: Don't fool yourself. If you're a late sleeper, avoid signing up for morning classes if at all possible. And if the registration computer gives you a morning class you didn't ask for, seriously consider changing it. Why make yourself miserable and risk a low or failing grade as well?

Some textbooks are overpriced. Some are extremely overpriced.

Students are a captive market. If your instructor assigns the textbook *Chemistry in Six Hundred Profusely Illustrated Pages* to your class, that's the textbook you have to use. Publishers are acutely aware of this, and price their books accordingly. A slim paperback text can thus run $20–25; a thick introductory text with color illustrations can easily run $45–$75. A term's worth of books can cost a full-time student $250–$500.

Solution 1: Buy textbooks used. Used texts are available through the following sources:

• Your college bookstore (particularly at the beginning and end of each term).

• Other bookstores near your college.

• Book sales and swaps. These are held for the specific purpose of buying and selling used textbooks. Book swaps are usually held at the beginning and/or end of the term, either at the college bookstore or the student union.

• Other students. People often put up signs offering to sell their used textbooks cheaply. Check campus bulletin boards, particularly those in the student union. Also check the classified ads in your college newspaper.

Solution 2: Don't own, borrow: Check the books you need out of libraries. You can probably find thirty to forty percent of the textbooks you need in your college library and/or other libraries. Check your college library first. If that doesn't work, try the public libraries (particularly the main branches of big-city libraries) and/or other college libraries in your area.

Some libraries have a computer data base which can tell you

exactly what titles are available throughout the city, county, or metropolitan area. These can locate any title for you quickly—or let you know if it is unavailable locally.

If a book you need is not available locally, you can order it through your college library's interlibrary loan desk. Books usually take two to six weeks to arrive. Interlibrary loan is often free, though some libraries charge a twenty-five cent to a dollar service charge per book.

Important: Many textbooks come in a variety of editions. When borrowing a textbook or buying a used one, always try to get the same edition that will be used in your class. If the same edition is not available, ask your instructor if a different edition will do; sometimes it will and sometimes it won't.

Solution 3: Many instructors put copies of required books on reserve in the college library. You can take reserve books out for two to twelve hours at a time (though at some schools reserve books cannot leave the library). You can also, of course, photocopy portions of reserve books to read at your leisure. If your instructor does not automatically put copies of texts on reserve, ask him to.

The big drawback of using reserve books is that other students may check them out before you. This is especially likely—and especially problematic—toward the end of the term.

Solution 4: Sell your textbooks when you're done with them, through one or more of the methods described above. This enables you to recoup some of the cost of textbooks each term. Often a book that you bought used can be sold yet again, perhaps for the same price you paid for it.

Your college bookstore may be sold out of some of the textbooks you need.

Some college bookstores, for reasons that I still don't understand, often order too few texts; for a course with an enrollment limit of thirty, for example, they'll order twenty-five. By the time you get to the store to buy your books, some of them may therefore be completely sold out.

Solution 1: Buy your textbooks as soon as possible—if you can, before the term begins or on the first day. If you are not sure whether you will be taking a certain class, buy the texts for it anyway; if you don't take the class, simply return the books for a full refund. (Be sure to keep them in new and unmarked condition, so that the bookstore will take them back.)

Solution 2: As soon as you learn that a book is sold out, let your instructor know. (Do *not* wait until the next class meeting; get hold of her during her office hours—or, if she has listed her home phone number on your syllabus, call her at home.) She will immediately instruct the bookstore to order more copies.

In the meantime, ask your teacher if she can loan you a copy of the text until the new copies arrive. If she can't or won't, ask her to either put a copy on reserve in the library or photocopy the reading assignments for the first week or two and send them to you.

Solution 3: Locate a copy of the book through one of the sources discussed in the previous section.

Solution 4: Check the bookstore again every day or two. Some students may drop the course and return their textbooks, which will then be put back on the shelf for sale.

Many textbooks are dull, wordy, and badly written—including some textbooks for writing classes.

About half the textbooks on the market are decently written and reasonably easy to read. An equal number are boring, confusing, or downright unintelligible.

Solution 1: Before you take any class—or at the very least, during the first week of the term—look at all the books and other required reading. If the reading looks like it will be extremely slow, difficult, or dull, consider taking a different course or section. Look at the texts for those other sections and courses, too, of course, to see if they are any better.

Solution 2: If you decide to (or have to) take a course with dreadful reading material, expect your studying to go slowly. Schedule sufficient studying time to enable you to wade through the awful prose. When anything is unclear or confusing (and expect much of it to be), ask your instructor for clarification or help.

Once the term is over, let your instructor know how difficult the reading was, and suggest that he assign something different in the future.

In some cases, your textbook and your instructor may contradict each other.

This happens fairly often. Sometimes it's a matter of two legitimate but different points of view or approaches; sometimes, though, one source is out of date or just plain incorrect.

Solution: Take the same general approach that you would if you were taught contradictory things in two different classes. Meet with your teacher in her office; bring your textbook with you. Bring up the contradiction in a polite, friendly, nonconfrontational way, and show her the questionable passage(s).

Pretending to understand something you don't won't help you, and will often get you into trouble.

No one wants to look stupid, and it can be embarrassing to have to raise your hand and say, "I'm sorry, but I just don't follow you. Could you explain that again?" It is extremely tempting to just sit quietly and hope to catch up or figure things out later.

Unfortunately, when people do remain silent, they tend to compound their problem. The teacher moves on to the next topic, which frequently builds on the very material that was confusing or unclear. The result: Things are even more confusing and unclear than before—and asking for help becomes twice as embarrassing.

Solution: When you don't understand something, say so. Come right out and ask for an explanation or clarification.

As you get used to doing this, it will get easier and easier. In the meantime, if admitting in class that you're confused seems too risky, wait until afterward, or speak to your instructor privately in his office.

Many students don't realize that it is quite possible to ask for further explanation without sounding ignorant. For example, you might say, "Could you run through the part about states' rights again?" or "I understand most of what you've said about centrifugal force—but could you review the key points of centripedal force one more time?" By saying what you *do* understand and making it clear that you have been listening and following some of what the teacher has said, you end up sounding not ignorant but intelligent.

The fact is that most teachers *welcome* questions and are happy to answer them, no matter how elementary they may be. Furthermore, if you're not following something, ninety percent of the time several other students aren't getting it, either—but they're too chicken to admit it. If you break the ice by saying, "Could you go over that again?" you do both yourself and your fellow students a favor.

Your college may not offer all the courses you want or need.

No college can offer a sufficient range of courses to suit every student. But as an informed student, you can still get what you want even if it's not listed in the regular class schedule.

Solution 1: If your college doesn't offer something you want, do an independent study in it. Virtually all universities and liberal arts colleges, and some other colleges as well, allow students to design their own independent study projects and earn academic credit for them. Usually all you need is a faculty sponsor—and finding one is normally just a matter of making a few phone calls and/or knocking on a few instructors' doors. For complete details on arranging an independent study, check your college's catalog or call your dean's office.

Solution 2: Do an internship in the field. There is no better way to learn than on-the-job, hands-on training, and that's exactly what internships provide. They usually carry academic credit, and sometimes pay a salary to boot. (If your school does not award academic credit for internships, try calling yours an independent study instead.)

There are two ways to arrange an internship. You can apply to fill an opening in an established internship program, or you can set up an internship on your own.

Notices of internship opportunities are often posted near the appropriate department office. A notice for an internship in broadcasting, for example, would normally be posted near the communications or radio/TV department office. Some colleges and universities also have separate internship offices that coordinate many internship opportunities.

If you prefer, you can set up your own internship. This isn't as difficult or uncommon as it sounds; all you need is a faculty member who is willing to sponsor you and an organization that is willing to put you to work. Many students have arranged internships on their own just by contacting a few organizations that interested them. A few phone calls, a little probing and networking, and an interview or two are often all it takes.

Solution 3: Take the class or classes you want at another college, and transfer in the credits. Some colleges permit cross-registration (registration for courses at other nearby colleges) at no extra charge; check with your registration office for details.

Solution 4: Transfer to another college.

Taking any class immediately after work, or during any period when your level of energy or attention is low, can cause problems. Taking more than two classes in a row (unless one of them is a fun, easy class) can also be very difficult.

With few exceptions, college classes require steady attention and mental energy. If, because of exhaustion, overwork, or your body cycles, you cannot bring the necessary energy and attention to a course, that course is going to be very tough for you.

Solution: Don't push yourself too hard. The simple fact is that after two academic classes in a row or several hours at a job, it is very hard to keep up your energy or focus your attention.

Plan your schedule so that it doesn't exhaust you. After work or two academic classes in a row, give yourself at least an hour to relax, exercise, meditate, eat a leisurely meal, or do something else you enjoy before heading into the classroom. This break will help you refresh yourself and recoup your energy, so that you will be alert, comfortable, and ready to learn.

Be aware of your energy levels, too; try not to schedule a difficult class during those hours when your energy typically runs low.

All of this can make a much bigger difference in what you learn, and in what grades you earn, than you may realize.

If you fall more than two weeks behind in a class, your chances of catching up are slim.

Once you are far enough behind in a course—or sufficiently lost or confused by the material—it is next to impossible to catch up again. For most people and most classes, this point of no return is about two weeks behind.

Solution: If and when you reach this point, the sanest thing to do in most cases is drop the class, or change your status in it to an auditor.

Struggling to catch up once you pass this point is usually a waste of your time and energy. At best you may sneak by with a barely passing grade; at worst, you'll flunk.

If you find yourself in this situation, *do not ask the instructor whether you should drop out of the course or stay in it.* Virtually every college teacher in the universe will urge you to stick with the course; but eighty-five percent of the time this will be bad advice. Most students who do stay enrolled fall further behind, do poorly in the class, and then must face the indignity of being told, "It's your own fault."

Remember, you can almost always take the class again later if you wish. And if you do take it again, you'll go into it with some previous experience—experience that will help you succeed on your second try.

Getting out before things get worse is particularly important in any subject which you plan to study further, so that you don't make your difficulties worse later. For example, if you're having serious trouble in Spanish 101, and you drop the course and repeat it later, you have a reasonable chance of doing well in it the second time, and perhaps even enjoying it. But if you stick with it, struggle through, and manage to pass with a D, you not only have a D on your record, but you are ill-prepared for Spanish 102! Enjoying or even passing Spanish 102 under these circumstances is just short of impossible.

Most colleges will allow you to drop courses without the penalty of a low grade until at least the middle of the term; some will let you drop classes up until the week of final exams. A dropped course will either not appear on your transcript at all, or will appear with the harmless grade of W, for "withdrawn."

Important: dropping below a certain number of credits may affect your financial aid status. If you are receiving financial aid, check with your college's financial aid office for specifics before dropping a class in midterm. Some of the most selective and prestigious colleges also require students to complete a minimum number of credits or courses per term in order to remain in good academic standing; consult your college catalog or check with your registration office for details.

10

Papers

Instructors won't always tell you what they want in a paper. Sometimes they don't really know what they want themselves. Other instructors have a clear idea of exactly what they want, but are unwilling or unable to articulate it.

Some teachers, particularly those in the humanities, will give you very vague writing assignments such as "I'd like a ten-page paper on the Crimean War" or "Write down your thoughts on Steinbeck in an organized and cogent manner."

In part, such vagueness can actually be a plus, since it gives you plenty of approaches to choose from. But it can also leave you wondering what to do and wishing you had further guidance.

Solution 1: Ask the instructor for clarification and/or more details. Feel free to say quite bluntly, "What are you looking for in this paper?" or "What are you expecting us to demonstrate in this assignment?" If his answers still leave you confused, ask him to give you some examples of themes, ideas, or approaches that he would find appealing.

If the teacher has not specified a length for the paper, ask for some general guidelines. If he dodges the question, or says something like "Start at the beginning and continue until the end," don't let the matter drop. Respond with, "Are you thinking of two pages? Five? Ten? Twenty?" This should coax him into giving you a useful answer.

Solution 2: Come up with three to five ideas for responses to the

132

assignment. You don't have to sketch them out in detail; simply knowing your central topic, premise, or approach will do. Write these all down; better yet, type them up.

Then meet with your teacher during his office hours or by appointment. Explain that you've come up with several ideas for the assignment and aren't sure which one to go with. Run them all by your instructor; then ask what he thinks of them and which one sounds most promising.

Your instructor will probably pick one or two of your ideas, which the two of you can then discuss and refine. But if he says, "All of those ideas sound good," that's great, too.

If none of your ideas pleases your instructor, respond this way: "I think I haven't really understood the assignment. Can you help me get on the right track?" This should get you some answers and assistance.

Two different instructors—even two instructors teaching different sections of the same course—might grade papers very differently.

It's hard to grade some papers scientifically, particularly papers for humanities courses. In the end, each instructor must often rely on her best overall judgment for giving grades. This judgment naturally varies quite a bit from one instructor to the next. Indeed, the same instructor's judgment can change a little from day to day, along with her mood, energy level, and circumstances.

But differences in judgment usually result in relatively small differences in grading. What makes a much bigger difference are the criteria each instructor uses to assign grades. For example, one sociology teacher may grade entirely on the basis of content, or on your demonstrated understanding and use of key sociological concepts. Another teacher may weigh the strength and intelligence of your overall argument just as heavily. A third may consider both of these elements, and give equal weight to your writing style as well.

Is any one of these sets of criteria better or more correct than any other? No. Will these three different instructors grade papers differently? Absolutely—in some cases very differently.

The greatest variation in grading often occurs in writing courses, particularly freshman composition. Teacher A might be primarily concerned with the overall effect of the entire paper. Teacher B might focus primarily or entirely on technical correctness: proper sentence structure, punctuation, word choice, spelling, and so on. Teacher C might be most concerned with your eloquence and your ability to persuade. Teacher D might care about all of the above.

Solution: Make no assumptions about an instructor's criteria for grading. When any teacher gives you your first writing assignment of the term, ask her, "What criteria do you use for grading papers?" or "What do you consider when reading and grading papers?" If necessary, ask her to be specific about what concerns her and what does not.

You must know what your teacher looks for, and what she considers important and unimportant, in order to write successful papers for her. If your instructor does not volunteer this information in class, and/or include it in the syllabus, you must ask her for it directly.

Occasionally the criteria by which a teacher actually assigns grades may be different from the criteria she claims to use. Once you get your first paper back with a grade on it, you will have a better idea of what the instructor genuinely thinks is important.

If you believe the grade you have received is inappropriate or unfair, there are several things you can do to appeal it. See pages 148–150 for details.

Many teachers grade according to spelling, grammar, style, and other items besides content.

Some teachers believe that every college student should learn good writing skills, and should demonstrate them in every paper they turn in. These teachers grade accordingly.

Solution 1: Write each paper as well as you can. Rewrite as much as necessary, edit the paper carefully, and, before handing it in, proofread it twice.

Solution 2: Almost every college and university in North America has a writing lab (sometimes called a writing center or study skills center), where tutors will help you with your writing at no charge.

Once you've gotten your paper in the best shape that you can, bring it to the writing lab and have a tutor go through it with you. Most tutors won't correct all of your technical problems, but they will point many of them out for you, and they'll either give you a crash course in the writing principles you need to learn or refer you to available books, work sheets, or tapes that will help you to quickly learn them on your own. If you're making the same type of mistake over and over, they'll let you know about it and show you how to keep from making it in the future.

Some writing labs require students to make appointments in advance, but most are open on a walk-in basis. To locate the writing lab at your college, call the English department office or the college operator.

A tutor in the writing lab can also help when you're having trouble in the early or intermediate steps of writing a paper.

Solution 3: If you have a friend or acquaintance who writes well, ask him to edit and proofread your work for you. You may want to trade him a service or favor in return.

Be sure to edit and proofread each paper yourself before giving it to anyone else; this ensures that the paper will be as polished as possible—and you will get valuable editing and proofreading practice in the process.

Important: It is unethical to have anyone else do any significant amount of writing for you. If someone else makes corrections and rewrites a sentence for you here and there, that's fine; but anything more than this borders on fraud. Stick within the legal and ethical limits.

Solution 4: Hire a good editor to edit and proofread your papers for you. Graduate students in English, creative writing, and journalism are your best bets.

To find an editor, post signs on bulletin boards near the English, journalism, and/or creative writing department offices. These might say, "Graduate student with excellent editing skills wanted to help edit and proofread papers. Pay negotiable. Call 555-6098."

You should be able to hire a graduate student for ten to twelve dollars per hour, though up to fifteen dollars an hour is reasonable. As noted above, make sure that you stick within the moral and legal limits for getting outside help.

Solution 5: Do your writing on a computer or word processor that has a spelling-check program. This will not help with sentence structure, punctuation, and other technical concerns, however, so use at least one of the other solutions above as well. (There are now some programs on the market that help with grammar, punctuation, and style, but none of them is all that good. Use one if you wish, but don't rely too heavily on it. A skilled human being will always be better than a language-check program.)

Some instructors, consciously or unconsciously, will penalize you if your papers are not typed. Some also feel that all papers should look neat and professional, and will grade accordingly.

Many college teachers require all papers to be neatly typed or computer-printed, and simply won't accept handwritten work. But even those instructors who do accept handwritten work will usually give slightly higher grades to papers that are typed or computer-printed. It is also true that nest papers usually receive slightly higher grades than sloppy-looking ones.

In most cases, this isn't a conscious decision on the instructor's part. It's simply that neatly-typed papers are easier to read and look more like the work of a scholar or professional. Neat, typed papers thus may seem clearer, better researched, or more convincing and authoritative.

Solution: Hand in neatly typed or computer-printed material whenever possible—even if handwritten work is acceptable. If you use a computer printer, letter-quality work is preferable, since it's easier to read. (If you don't have a letter-quality printer, you can have your papers laser-printed at a nearby copy shop.)

If you can't type, *learn.* You will need this skill throughout your college career and for the rest of your life, so you might as well learn it as soon as possible.

If you're still in high school, take a typing class at your school. If you've already finished high school and will begin college in the fall, take an introductory typing course during the summer. Your local community college, technical college, or vocational school should offer a course at a very reasonable price, either as a standard offering or through its continuing education (also called community education, adult education, etc.) program. Inexpensive noncredit typing courses are also offered through community centers, continuing education programs sponsored by local public school systems, and other community and educational organizations. Business schools offer typing courses, too, but these can be expensive.

If you are already in college, take a typing course as soon as possible. If your college does not offer such a course, take one at one of the organizations listed above. In the meantime, pay someone to type your work for you. Check campus bulletin boards and the classifieds in your college newspaper for ads for professional typists. The going rate is $1.20–$1.75 per double-spaced page, $1.60–$2.30 in Canada. Be sure to give your typist sufficient advance notice so that she can fit you into her schedule. Also allow her enough time to get the typed paper to you at least one or two days ahead of your deadline; this gives you enough time to proofread the paper carefully, and, if necessary, have her correct any errors.

If you can already type, but cannot type neatly or reasonably accurately, spend the money to have someone else type your work for you. A sloppy or error-ridden paper will look bad and work against you, even if it's typed.

Many of your college papers will require rewriting, as well as plenty of time, effort, and research.

With few exceptions, college papers require hard work and genuine thought. Unlike the papers you may have written in high school, they cannot be thrown together at the last minute or written off the top of your head.

Solution: Give yourself plenty of time to think about, write, and rewrite each paper, plus adequate time to edit, proofread, and type it (or have it typed).

One excellent way to cut down on rewriting—and to improve your grades—is to bring a draft of your paper to your teacher a few days or weeks before it is due. Either make an appointment or stop by his office during his office hours. Show him what you have so far, explain that it is a draft, and ask if he will look it over, tell you if you're on the right track, and make suggestions for the final version. Most teachers will be happy to read and respond to your work on the spot—and most will be impressed by your effort and your purposefulness. Their comments on your draft will help you to improve your paper and tailor it more closely to what they want.

You may also bring interim drafts to any of the people who can do editing for you: a writing lab tutor, a skilled friend or acquaintance, or a hired graduate student. Any or all of these people may be able to offer useful comments and suggestions.

Another strategy is to *finish* your paper, except for editing and proofreading, and bring it to your instructor to read *as if it were a draft.* Ask for his comments and suggestions. If you're pretty much on the mark, he'll say, "This looks pretty good; it just needs some editing." If he doesn't like what he sees, he'll give you suggestions for improving it. This approach gives you the chance to get feedback on papers (and, if necessary, to rewrite them) before you hand them in.

Typists can and do make major mistakes, including those who use word processing equipment. Even if you pay your typist to proofread, your paper may still contain major typing errors.

I have never met a typist who was also a really good proofreader, no matter what equipment she had or what she claimed she could do.

Meanwhile, if you hand in a paper that has been poorly proofread and, as a result, has quite a few technical problems, it makes no difference whether the fault is yours or your typist's; you are still the one who will pay the price of a lower grade.

Solution: Always proofread all of your papers at least twice before handing them in. Do this *even if* someone else has typed and proofread your work for you.

When arranging to have your work typed, give the typist plenty of advance notice, as well as enough time to type it and get it back to you *no later than a day or two before the paper is due.* This gives you time to proofread the finished product—and, if anything needs correcting or retyping, it gives the typist time to make the necessary changes.

Papers sometimes vanish mysteriously between the time students turn them in and the time instructors are ready to read them.

Students think teachers lose their papers. Teachers think students fail to turn them in in the first place. Whatever the cause, one out of fifty papers somehow evaporates after it has been written.

Solution: Always—I repeat, *always,* with no exceptions—make a photocopy of every paper (or other assignment) you write before you turn it in. If the original disappears, give the teacher your photocopy.

But if this happens, before you turn in your photocopy, make another photocopy of it. Though it is very rare, it is possible for two copies of the same paper to disappear.

11

Tests and Exams

Two different teachers may grade the same test very differently. This may be the result of differing criteria for evaluation, differing standards, or both. This situation can occur not only with essay tests, but with multiple-choice and other objective tests as well.

Just as with grading papers, two different instructors may use very different criteria for grading essay exams. One may be concerned primarily or entirely with the knowledge and understanding that you demonstrate; a second may also be concerned with how cogently you present that information and how well you write; and a third may be concerned with all of these, and with spelling, grammar, and punctuation as well. Even when teachers do use the same criteria to assign grades, they may not share the same standards.

Standards can also play a part in the grading of objective tests. These tests may be graded according to the number of correct and incorrect answers; however, different instructors may have different views on what number of correct answers corresponds to each letter grade.

Imagine a test of 100 questions which two different instructors use in two different sections of the same course. One might decide that 92 or more correct answers merits an A, 84 or more a B, and 76 or more a C; the other might require 94 correct answers for an A, 88 or more for a B, and 82 or more for a C.

Further variation in grading can occur when instructors grade on a curve instead of setting objective standards. An instructor who grades on a curve might, for example, give A's to the top 10% of all test scores, B's to the next 15%, C's to the next 50%, D's to the next 15%, and F's to the lowest 10%. In a class of bright or well-prepared students, then, a score of 87 might earn a C; in a less sharp or well-prepared class, 87 might be worth a B.

Solution: There's nothing you can do to eliminate the variation in grading from teacher to teacher or course to course. You *can,* however, choose your teachers and courses carefully, using the tips in chapters 7 and 9.

Ultimately what's important is not what specific grading system a teacher uses, but whether that teacher tries to be as fair and reasonable as possible. If your teacher is reasonable, your grades will be, too.

If you receive a grade on any test or exam that you feel is *not* fair or reasonable, feel free to challenge it. Follow the guidelines on pages 148–150.

Some tests and exams don't genuinely test your knowledge or understanding of a subject. Some will test little or nothing more than your ability to memorize.

It's difficult to design a test that can truly evaluate your grasp of a subject rather than your ability to memorize a lot of information. This is one reason why many instructors have abandoned tests completely in favor of papers, oral presentations, and/or group projects.

Some instructors *have* managed to design some very useful essay tests. Others, who still use badly designed essay tests or objective tests, are well aware that their tests aren't very useful—but they are unwilling or unable to come up with anything better.

Solution: When a teacher uses tests as his sole or primary method of evaluating your progress, study for his class in two different ways: for yourself, and for each test.

From week to week, study for yourself. Concentrate on those ideas and topics that most intrigue you. Keep up with the class, but also let yourself pursue your own relevant interests.

But when you have a test coming up, switch gears temporarily. Focus only on that upcoming test, and on the specific material you'll need to memorize and comprehend for it.

Here are some tips that will help:

As you study for a test or exam, write down key terms, concepts, premises, and questions on a sheet of paper, along with appropriate definitions and/or notes. On a second sheet of paper, write down items you have trouble remembering or keeping clear in your mind. Every fifteen minutes or so, review both of these sheets. Reading them aloud to yourself helps; the concepts and spoken words will reinforce one another in your memory.

After you go through both pages each time, quiz yourself on them mentally. Repeat this process regularly until test time, or as close to test time as possible.

Students typically do much of their studying the night before the test. However, many students do better if they do only some of their studying the night before, then go to bed at a reasonable hour, get up very early in the morning (if necessary, in the middle of the night), and study right up until the test begins, or as close to that time as possible. This strategy limits the amount of information that drifts away during sleep. Studying right up until the exam also enables you to have the most information fresh in your mind.

If at all possible, do not drive to class on the day of the test. Have someone else drive you, or take public transportation. This enables you to study right up until the moment the test begins. Bring your pages of key concepts and things to remember with you; go through them periodically, either mentally or aloud (aloud usually works better), quizzing yourself afterward each time.

Arrive at the testing room ten minutes before the test begins, carrying these two pages with you. Go through them several more times outside the room until just before the test starts. Then put them away and enter the room.

As soon as you are given an exam book or scratch paper, quickly jot down the concepts that you feel will be most important and the ones you're most likely to forget. Once you've written these down, stop trying to remember them; simply refer to your notes as necessary.

Test questions will not always be clear, precise, unambiguous, or even understandable.

Teachers do not always spend the time and care that they should to consider, write, rewrite, and edit test questions. Furthermore, sometimes what is clear and unambiguous to them may not be to others.

I have never encountered a college teacher who deliberately wrote confusing test questions—but I have met quite a few who tried hard to be clear but weren't always able to.

Solution: As soon as you are given the questions for any essay test or exam, read them all carefully before beginning the test. If anything is unclear, or if anything can be taken in more than one way, immediately ask your teacher or proctor about it. If her answer is equally unclear, make no bones about saying, "It's still not clear to me. Could you say that in another way?" In the case of an ambiguous question, come right out and say, "This question can mean two different things. It can mean _____ [restate one possible meaning], or _____ [restate the other]. Which do you mean?"

It is extremely important that you speak up. If you do not fully understand a question, you may not be able to give the kind of answer the teacher is looking for—and you may do very badly on the test as a result. *Don't be embarrassed about asking for clarification.* Chances are that most of your fellow students are just as confused as you are.

If, after you have begun taking an essay or objective test, you realize a question is unclear or ambiguous, ask the teacher or proctor privately about it.

Teachers will not always give you enough time to take a test.

When preparing tests and exams, particularly essay tests, instructors do not always carefully consider how much time students will need to answer each question.

Solution: Always wear a watch when you take a test. Look at it frequently, and carefully pace yourself. Bring at least two pens or pencils with you; this saves you time and trouble in case a point breaks or a pen runs out of ink. Follow the following tips as well.

For multiple-choice and other objective tests:

As soon as you get your test, note the number of questions you have to answer and the total time you have to answer them all. Quickly calculate about how much time you have for each question. If you find yourself taking much more than this amount of time on any one question, skip it and move on.

Go through the questions rapidly from beginning to end, answering the ones you are sure of and the ones that don't take much time. Skip any questions that stump you, that you are undecided about, or that look like they'll take a good deal of time or thought. If you are fairly but not completely sure about an answer, put down that answer, and place a small dot next to it.

Then go back and quickly check the answers to the easy questions. If you are filling in a machine-graded answer sheet, make sure you have filled in the proper box or circle corresponding to your answer. Also check that each answer corresponds to the proper question. For example, if the answer to question 29 is D and you have skipped question 28 for the moment, make sure that you answer D on line 29, and not on line 28. This is worth double-checking.

Next, go through those questions that you think are correct but are not completely sure of. When you are reasonably sure of an answer, erase the dot next to it; if you are still uncertain, make your best guess and leave the dot in place. If you have time, you can come back to these questions later on.

Now go back to the beginning and go through the difficult questions again. Spend a little time on each one; but if you get nowhere or realize a question will take quite a bit of time, forget about it and move on.

When just a few minutes remain, go through all the questions very briefly once again, to check that you've answered them as best you can, and to make sure that you've filled in all the proper circles or boxes. Erase any remaining dots next to your answers. If any time still remains, look at the answers you are uncertain about one last time.

If your test will be graded only according to the number of answers you get right, answer every question. Give the best answer you can; if you can't choose between two options, guess; if you have no idea, also guess. If you do not have enough time to consider every question, give random answers to the remaining questions when you have one or two minutes left.

Although it is rare, some teachers grade tests according to the number of right answers *and* the number of wrong answers. For example, each correct answer might be worth one point; a wrong answer, however, instead of being worth nothing at all, might actually lower your score by, say, a quarter of a point. Most nationally standardized tests such as the ACT and SAT use this grading system. If there is a penalty for an incorrect answer, do *not* answer any question you are completely stumped by. However, if you can eliminate one or more of the choices, *do* make your best guess from among the other options.

If your instructor or proctor does not clearly state at the beginning of the test whether or not there is a penalty for a wrong answer, ask about it.

When taking essay tests, follow these guidelines:

As soon as you are given your list of questions, read them all carefully and make sure you understand them fully. Ask for clarification if necessary. If you can choose which question(s) to answer, spend the first few minutes considering all the questions and deciding which ones to respond to. You do not have to answer the questions in the order in which they are presented, so long as you clearly indicate in each answer which question you are answering. Some students like to answer the easiest questions first; this helps them build their confidence and momentum.

Budget your time carefully in advance. Set aside the final twenty to twenty-five percent of your time for editing, proofreading, and making corrections. Allot a specific amount of the remaining time for each question, allowing yourself more time for the longer or more difficult responses. For example, if you have two hours to take the test and four questions to answer, set aside the last half hour for editing and proofreading; of the remaining ninety minutes, you might allot fifteen minutes for one question and twenty-five for each of the three others. Jot down which questions you will answer and the amount of time you've given yourself for each one.

Pace yourself carefully, referring frequently to your watch. Don't go over your allotted time for any question by more than a few minutes. *It is always better to answer all the questions adequately than some extremely well and some poorly, hurriedly, incompletely, or haphazardly.*

Before you begin writing your answer to any question, look it over once again. Most students write their best responses if they spend a few minutes considering their response before starting to write. You may also find it helpful to outline your answer or jot down some notes or key points.

For each question, go through these steps:

• Formulate your response, either in your head, in notes, or in an informal outline.

• Write your response.

• Check your respone for clarity, completeness, and responsiveness to the question. Rewrite as necessary.

• During the last twenty to twenty-five percent of your time, edit and proofread all your responses.

In certain classes, performance on one or two tests may determine most or all of your final grade.

Some teachers base students' final grades for the term on the results of the final exam, plus one other item: a paper, an oral presentation, a group project, or a midterm exam. There's nothing educationally wrong with this, but it means that the results of your final exam—or your final exam and your midterm—can make or break you in the course.

Solution 1: From the beginning of the term, be prepared to spend a great deal of time studying for the final exam (and for the midterm, if there is one). Plan to study for at least two or three solid days before the final exam, doing little else except eating, sleeping, and attending your other classes. Plan to study for the midterm for at least one or two full days.

Don't treat this class like your other courses. Since so much is riding on one or two exams, you must put a disproportionate amount of your time into studying for them. Follow the advice on test-taking earlier in this chapter.

Solution 2: If courses that are based largely or entirely on final exam results frighten you or make you terribly anxious, don't take them. Look for a different course, section, or instructor instead.

When you interview teachers and get syllabi for their courses, look each syllabus over carefully. It should explain precisely how your final grade will be determined; if it doesn't, ask the instructor for details.

One section of a course may use tests to determine your final grade; another section may use papers instead; still another may use both.

As I explained earlier, each instructor usually has the right to determine the content, approach, and grading criteria for each course and section she teaches. Thus any two sections of the same course may differ markedly in how students are evaluated.

Solution: Never assume that different sections of the same course will be identical, or even terribly similar. Refer to the course syllabus to see exactly what the class will require in the way of papers, tests, oral presentations, and/or other projects. If the syllabus is not clear about this, ask the instructor for details.

12

Grades

Grades are not nearly as important to most students' future success, or to their lives in general, as most people think they are.

Most students, and many teachers and administrators, put far too much emphasis on grades. The truth is that grades have a very limited impact on most students' lives once they have left college.

While you're a college student, you obviously need passing grades in order to accumulate credits and eventually graduate. You may need a certain grade point average in order to play team sports, to join an honor society, or to get or keep certain forms of financial aid. Grades also make a difference if you plan to transfer to another college, apply for a postgraduate fellowship, or attend graduate, medical, or law school.

Beyond this, however, grades have very little meaning. Most employers won't care a bit about your college grades; they'll just want to know if you have the ability, experience, and/or degree necessary for the job. (One unsurprising exception: Colleges look carefully at the grades of people who want to be hired as instructors.)

Otherwise, no one (except perhaps your parents) is likely to care about your grades. Good grades won't guarantee you happiness, success, or the right job after you graduate. And how many times have you heard "I'm a straight-A student" used as a pickup line?

Since I received my B.A. in 1978, I do not believe a single person outside of academia has asked me what my college grades were. Even my wife doesn't care—and why in the world should she?

Solution: Keep grades in perspective. Use them as a measure of your success in individual courses, and nothing more. People build successful lives out of intelligence, hard work, planning, patience, luck, smart risk-taking, and good timing—not out of high grades. For every happy or successful person who had a high grade point average in college, there's another whose grades were mediocre or unexceptional.

In short, shoot for high grades, but don't knock yourself out or drive yourself crazy over them.

Some teachers give grades capriciously or arbitrarily. Some give higher grades to students they like or find attractive.

This will hardly be news to you, since many of your high school teachers probably did the same thing.

Actually, most college teachers grade quite fairly; only about twenty to twenty-five percent play favorites or let their emotions interfere with their judgment. Most of the time, an instructor's judgment is more likely to be slightly skewed by his mood, state of health, or lack of patience than by overt favoritism.

All sorts of other things probably have a minor effect, too: the weather, the time of day, the paper or test he just graded a few moment ago, and so on.

Solution: First of all, don't concern yourself with what grades other students get—it's a complete waste of energy. If you get a B − in your literature course and the attractive woman who did almost no work gets an A, don't try to get *her* grade changed. That's none of your business, and it won't work, anyway. Instead, focus on whether or not the grade *you* received is fair.

If you believe a grade you received—for a test, a paper, an oral presentation, some other project, or an entire course—is inappropriate or unfair, don't just stew about it. *It is often possible to get your grade changed if you can make a good case for changing it.* Here's what to do:

Make an appointment with the instructor, or visit him during his office hours. Bring the paper, test, or project in question with you; if you plan to challenge your grade for the entire course, bring all of your tests, papers, and/or projects for the term. *Save all of these items throughout the term in the event that you need them for just such an occasion.*

Arrive at your instructor's office neatly groomed, neatly dressed, and on time. Throughout your discussion, remain polite and calm—but also be willing to be assertive. Don't let the teacher bully you or talk over you. Insist politely that your case be heard.

Begin by explaining that you want to discuss your grade. Don't say yet that you think it's wrong or unfair, just that you want to talk about it.

Next, check to make sure that the grades your instructor has in his grade book match those on your tests and/or papers. Five percent of the time they won't, and you have solved your problem right then and there.

If the grades do match, ask the instructor what method or formula he used to determine them. Make sure you understand this formula clearly and completely; if you don't, press your teacher for an explanation. Then ask him to go through your work again right then, applying that method once more, to make sure that he arrives at the same grade he gave you before.

For example, if you are challenging the grade on a paper, ask the instructor to go through the paper with you, explaining its strengths and weaknesses. If you're challenging your final grade for the term, ask your teacher to go through the process of averaging out all your grades on tests, projects, papers, etc., with you. Sometimes he will come up with a different grade than the one he originally gave you.

If everything checks out so far and your grade remains unchanged, you have three options: (1) accept the grade you have been given; (2) challenge the teacher's method or formula for grading; or (3) explain why your circumstances are unusual, and thus your work should not be subject to the regular grading formula.

Option 2 does not work very often—but if you truly believe your instructor's method of grading is unfair, make your best and most reasonable case as to why it is unfair. Remember to remain calm and polite at all times.

Option 3 also succeeds only rarely—but if your situation is genuinely unusual in some way, let the teacher know.

Do not try any of the following strategies, as they are doomed to failure: whining, pleading, accusations, comparisons with other teachers ("Dr. Black would have given me a B for this"), comparisons with other students ("But you gave the woman with the long red hair an A"), near-miss rationalizations ("But it's only half a point from being a C"), pronouncements of impending doom ("Now I'll never get into med school"), or guilt trips ("I'll never get into med school and it will be all your fault").

If none of the above strategies succeeds, and you still believe strongly that you have received an unfair grade, take your case to your dean.

One final note on this subject: Since grades aren't all-important in the first place, it's probably not worthwhile to try to get a B changed to a B+, a C− changed to a C, etc. Save your energy for battles that are truly worth fighting.

Grades do not necessarily reflect your ability, understanding, knowledge, interest, or wisdom in a subject.

Grades mostly reflect your ability to perform according to whatever criteria and/or tests your instructor has set up. It's possible, for example, to get an A in an introductory sociology class without fully comprehending the basic concepts and premises of sociology. It's also possible to flunk that same class but learn an enormous amount about the subject in the process.

Letter grades are an extremely coarse and inaccurate measure of anyone's learning. *Usually* a high grade means you've learned quite a bit, and a low grade means you've learned little. But exceptions to this general rule abound.

Solution: If you've gotten an A—or even straight A's—in a subject, don't assume you're an expert in it. Congratulate yourself for doing well, but don't forget that you still have a great deal more to learn about it. There may even be entirely different approaches to (and viewpoints on) the subjects that you don't know about.

And if you've gotten a poor grade, this doesn't mean you haven't learned anything. Ask yourself what you *did* learn and did get out of the course.

As before, if you feel the grade you have received is unfair, speak to your instructor about it.

Incompletes may cause more problems than they solve.

If you are unable to complete all of the work for a course by the end of the term, you have the option of extending your deadline beyond the end of the term and receiving a temporary grade of I, for incomplete. Your instructor's permission is required for this, and she may set whatever new deadline for turning in the work that she chooses. Once you complete all the required work, your instructor grades it and assigns you a final grade for the term; the I on your record is then replaced with this final grade.

All of this sounds great in theory. In practice, however, it creates problems more often than it solves them, because it doesn't eliminate any work—all it does is postpone it until later. And if you do not turn in all the required work by your new deadline, you flunk the course.

This is exactly what happens much of the time. Of the students who have taken incompletes in my courses over the years, the great majority of them have had their incompletes turn into F's.

When students arrange for incompletes, they don't usually consider how or when they will find the extra time to make up the work. Finding this extra time isn't easy. In theory you can always catch up during the following term—but in practice this almost never works. During the following term you're going to be busy with *that* term's work—and if you didn't have the time to do a full term's work last time around, how are you going to find the time to do a full term's work *plus* the additional makeup work in the term to come?

In the end, then, taking an incomplete often means giving yourself a next-to-impossible task—and setting yourself up for failure.

Solution 1: Avoid incompletes as much as possible. If you absolutely must have some extra time, ask your instructor for an extension until just before she must assign final grades. This will give you some extra time without your having to take an incomplete.

Solution 2: If *and only if* you simply cannot finish the work for the course by the time final grades are due, ask the instructor for an incomplete—*but ask her to set an unconditional deadline of the day before the beginning of the next term.* This frees you from having to deal with making up work during the following term, and thus minimizes your chances of flunking the course.

Solution 3: Take an incomplete and do the remaining work for the course during the following term—but either take that term off or take a reduced course load. To ensure that you complete all the makeup work, deliberately include it as part of your regular schedule.

Although they are a very small minority, a few instructors may offer to trade you a high grade for sex—or may threaten you with a low grade if you withhold sex from them.

These people are the scum of academia. Recent public awareness, court cases, and dismissals have reduced their numbers somewhat; however, some of them are still teaching.

Some of these instructors make their threats and offers quite bluntly, as if they were making business deals. Others, however, are more subtle, and use gestures, innuendo, or implication to get their message across. For example, a teacher might call you into his office, tell you how poorly you are doing in his course, and then point to his crotch and say, "But I'm sure you can bring your grade up if you really work hard."

This is all quite deliberate; if confronted, the teacher can claim that he said nothing unusual, and that you must have imagined the pointing finger.

The great majority of these teachers are men, and most of the students they practice their sleazy behavior on are women. However, male teachers have tried these tactics on male students, and female teachers have tried them with both men and women.

Solution: Absolutely refuse to tolerate such behavior from any teacher.

If an instructor uses grades to try to have sex with you, leave his office immediately. As promptly as possible, write down exactly what he said and did, and note the day and time. Then make the earliest appointment that you can with your dean. Explain to the secretary when you make the appointment exactly what you need to talk with the dean about.

Do not return to the instructor's class. Type up your notes from your unfortunate meeting. Make and keep a copy for yourself; bring the other with you to the dean's office.

At your appointment with the dean, explain in detail exactly what happened, and give him your typed notes. Insist that you be permitted to withdraw from the instructor's class without financial or academic penalty. You have several options here: You may ask to transfer into a different section or course, to drop the course and receive a full refund, to complete the course as an independent study with a different instructor, or to be given full credit and a grade for the course by another teacher. (This last option is only viable during the last two or three weeks of the term.)

If you wish, also insist that the instructor be brought before a review board. Let the dean know that you wish to file an official complaint against the instructor, and ask how to do so.

The great majority of deans will be sympathetic, and will do everything they can for you. In fact, in most cases, your complaint will be only one of several they have received against your instructor.

However, a very few misguided deans, in an attempt to avoid scandal, may try to brush your complaint aside or doubt your word about what happened; they may even defend the instructor. (The standard defense is, "Think carefully about what you're doing. The teacher has a family and a career. Do you really want to ruin all these lives over one little incident?") If any of this happens, leave the dean's office *immediately*. Write down what the dean said and did; then make an appointment with your provost. At this appointment, ask to file a formal complaint against both the instructor *and* the dean. You may also wish to sue the college.

If your instructor uses a subtle or implied approach to pressure you into having sex with him, don't let that stop you from going to your dean. Although you may have no clear, overt evidence, most deans will take your complaint very seriously. Chances are that they have gotten similar reports about the instructor from several other students.

13

Graduation Requirements

Graduation requirements can differ enormously from one college to another. They can even differ greatly from one school to another within the same university.

North American colleges have no uniform standards for degrees. St. John's College in New Mexico, for example, has a long list of specific courses that all students must take. Brown University has virtually no specific course requirements at all. Metropolitan State University not only has few course requirements, but requires all students to design their own academic programs.

In general, liberal arts colleges have the fewest specific graduation requirements; community, vocational, technical, and business colleges the most; and universities and junior colleges somewhere in between. Art colleges, music conservatories, institutes of technology, and other highly specialized schools tend to require a moderate to high number of specific courses for graduation.

Most liberal arts colleges and universities have what is called a distribution requirement, which mandates that each student study in three or more general academic areas in order to graduate. Usually these general areas are the sciences, the humanities (history, literature, languages, etc.), and the social sciences. Students may choose the courses they wish within these areas.

Overall, however, there is no consensus on what should or should not be required for a college degree.

Nor is there a consensus on what is necessary to complete any specific major. At one college, an English major may be required to complete a strict array of ten specific courses; at another, an English major may only have to complete seven literature courses of his or her choice, plus one required course in Shakespeare. Some colleges do not require (or, in some cases, permit) students to choose a major at all.

On top of this, even the titles of degrees can vary from school to school. Community and junior colleges usually award the Associate of Arts and Associate of Science degrees, but some offer unusual variations as well, such as the Associate of Applied Arts and the Associate of Applied Science. Four-year colleges and universities usually award the Bachelor of Arts and/or Bachelor of Science degrees; but over a dozen other variations exist, such as the Bachelor of General Studies, the Bachelor of Applied Science, the Bachelor of Fine Arts, the Bachelor of Music, the Bachelor of Education, and the Bachelor of Engineering. There are over thirty different types of graduate degrees as well.

Solution: When you begin researching colleges, think carefully about how much freedom—and how much responsibility—you want in choosing courses and designing your own academic program. If being able to chart your own course is important to you, or if you already know exactly what you want to do in college, look for schools that allow you considerable flexibility in course selection, and/or those that let you design your own program. But if the discipline and sense of community that come from following a closely structured academic program appeal to you, look into colleges like St. John's. If you don't yet know what your strongest educational interests are, and want guidance but not a lockstep program, then look at traditional universities, liberal arts colleges, and/or community colleges.

Most college catalogs describe all of their degree requirements in some detail in the section entitled Degree Programs or Academic Programs. Each different degree will have different requirements. Within large universities, each college or school—for instance the college of liberal arts, the school of nursing, the institute of technology, etc.—will have its own programs, majors, and degree requirements.

If you know what your major is likely to be, it is also an excellent idea to find out the requirements for that major. Call the appropriate department office and ask to be sent a description of the major that interests you. Also ask to be sent a copy of the department handbook, if one is available. (College catalogs often list requirements for specific majors, but these listings are frequently out of date or inaccurate; only information that comes directly from the appropriate department is sure to be correct.)

If designing your own program or having a great deal of academic flexibility interests you, good places to begin your college research are John Bear's books: *Bear's Guide to Earning Non-Traditional Degrees* (Ten Speed Press, 1988) and *College Degrees By Mail* (Ten Speed Press, 1990). These excellent books describe most of the nontraditional colleges and programs in North America, and the options they offer. The books also evaluate each college and program—a necessity, since some of the colleges that offer self-designed degrees are essentially fraudulent organizations that sell worthless degrees to anyone willing to spend money for them.

Many traditional colleges and universities offer a design-your-own-program option *in addition to* their standard degree programs. Usually this program is administered through an office known as Self-Designed Degrees, University Without Walls, or something similar. The University of Minnesota offers *two* such programs, one called University College and the other called Program for Individualized Learning. At some colleges, designing your own program is an option open only to honors students.

A few colleges, such as Norwich University's Vermont College, offer legitimate, accredited degree programs which do not even require you to be on campus most of the year. These schools allow students to complete their degrees primarily through independent study, under the close supervision of one or more instructors. Only highly motivated and self-directed students are normally admitted.

Your college's graduation requirements may be extremely lengthy, complex, or difficult to fulfill. Some schools have so many graduation requirements that they leave students with little or no time to pursue their own academic interests.

There's nothing wrong with being given direction—as long as that direction is appropriate to your own goals, needs, and interests. But if you find that your school's graduation requirements are keeping you from pursuing your educational interests, your situation needs to be changed.

Solution 1: Try to avoid this situation in the first place by wisely and carefully selecting the colleges you apply to. Follow the tips earlier in this chapter.

Solution 2: If your college's rules don't help further your education, you may be able to get some of them waived. Consider the advice on pages 73–74.

Solution 3: See if your college has a design-your-own-program option. Call your dean's office or check your college catalog for details.

Solution 4: If your current college doesn't offer what you need, or its rules make getting what you need difficult or impossible, transfer to another college. If you attend a large university, you might even be able to find what you need at another school within that same university.

Transferring is neither difficult nor dishonorable; in fact, about ten percent of all students transfer from one college to another. The application process is nearly identical to the process of applying for freshman admission. Before you officially transfer anywhere, however, be sure that most of the college credits you've earned so far will transfer (see page 79 for details). Transferring can also affect your financial aid status, either positively or negatively. Check with each college's financial aid office for specific information.

Some graduation requirements may seem arbitrary. Some may be downright silly or absurd.

As I explained in chapter 4, many college rules are established for reasons having little or nothing to do with education. Internal politics, state law, educational fads, departmental fighting, and half a dozen other strange forces may play a part.

Solution 1: Try to have an exception made. See pages 73–74.

Solution 2: See if a self-designed degree option is available.

Solution 3: Transfer elsewhere.

Solution 4: Ignore the apparent arbitrariness, silliness, or absurdity, and sign up for the required courses. If you choose your instructors carefully, according to the suggestions in chapter 7, you may find these classes interesting and worthwhile—and perhaps even exciting. In the end, the requirements may no longer seem so arbitrary, silly, or absurd at all.

The graduation requirements established by your college and/or major department may change between the time you first enroll and the time you are a senior. They may even change more than once.

Because there is so little national or international consensus on what constitutes a college education, nearly every college's graduation requirements are constantly under fire—from teachers, administrators, alumni, trustees, parents, educational theorists, and a wide range of other folks. As a result, most colleges tinker with their graduation requirements every year or two—sometimes in an effort to genuinely improve their students' educations, sometimes to appease certain vocal critics, and sometimes simply to give the impression that something significant is being done.

Solution: As I discussed on page 72, the graduation requirements that were in effect at the time you first enrolled in a college are the ones that continue to apply to you until you graduate—regardless of how radically or often those requirements may change. Even if you have taken a leave of absence, and/or have dropped out and reenrolled, those same requirements that were in effect when you first enrolled normally continue to apply to you.

However, if graduation requirements have gotten more lenient since you first enrolled, you may wish to go to your dean and ask to have these new requirements applied to you. Normally you'll need to give the dean a good reason to grant your request; but if a considerable amount of time has passed—say, three or more years—since the new requirements were instituted, you may be able to convince the dean to apply them to you just by saying, "Most of the other students here are subject to these rules; why shouldn't I be?"

The question of majors and minors is a bit different. The requirements for any major or minor that are in effect *at the time you declare that major* are the ones that continue to apply to you, even if the rules are later changed. Taking a leave of absence, or dropping out and reenrolling, does not affect these requirements. Again, however, if the rules become easier, you may be able to talk the powers that be (in this case, the department head instead of the dean) into letting you follow the new rule.

Note: If graduation requirements do change while you are a student, I strongly recommend that you visit your registration office about a month before your scheduled graduation day. Ask to go over your academic record with someone in the registration office to make sure that all your requirements are (or will soon be) complete and that everything looks in order. *Let the registration staff person know that the previous graduation requirements apply to you;* if necessary, explain those requirements to her. If she was initially unaware of the earlier requirements or the fact that they apply to you, ask her to attach a note to your record explaining the situation.

Your college may require you to take a basic math, reading, and/or writing class in addition to its regularly required math and writing courses. These basic courses may carry little or no college credit.

Colleges expect all new students to have attained a certain level of skill in reading, writing, and math. In many cases, you will need these skills to be able to pass even introductory-level courses. Many colleges therefore offer basic (also called "remedial") classes in reading, writing, and math for students whose skills are not yet up to the required level. These courses usually have titles such as Basic English, Refresher Math, Fundamentals of Reading, and so on, and they usually have course numbers under 100. Some of these classes carry academic credit, but some do not.

If your college has reason to believe that your skills in one or more of these areas are not up to par, you may be required to take one or more basic classes during your first term. Usually you will not be permitted to take any more advanced class in writing or math until you have successfully completed the basic course in the subject.

At many schools, credits for basic courses may not be counted toward a degree. Basic courses also may normally not be applied toward any major, and may not be used to fulfill any distribution or graduation requirements. For example, if your college requires all students to pass two math courses to graduate, your basic math class will not count as one of those two classes.

Solution 1: If your skills in reading, math, and/or writing are genuinely weak, normally the smart thing to do is take the basic class(es) you're assigned to. These classes will give you the solid background you need to be able to succeed in college; without them, making progress may be next to impossible. Be sure to find the best instructor for each course that you can.

Solution 2: If you have been told to take a basic class, but nevertheless feel that your skills in that area are perfectly adequate, follow these guidelines:

First, find out exactly how the college determined that you need to take a basic class. Your advisor should be able to tell you; the office of the appropriate department (English, math, study skills, etc.) should also have this information.

Colleges may assign you to a basic class based on your high school grades, your ACT or SAT scores, the results of a college-administered placement exam (the most likely possibility), or some combination of these. Find out exactly what information the college used to make its judgment; then find out what your own score is, and what the standard cutoffs are. For example, if your college uses a statewide math placement exam, find out what score you received, *and* what score you would need to get out of having to take a basic course.

If your score is significantly below the cutoff, chances are good that a basic class makes sense for you. However, if your score came reasonably close, or if you still believe strongly that you already have the necessary skills, you can appeal the decision to place you in a basic class.

I know of no college that offers basic courses that does not also offer a test for placing out of each of those courses. If you were placed in a basic class partly or entirely because of your score on such an exam, ask to take that exam again. If such an exam was *not* used to place you in the basic course, ask to take it now and to be assigned to a class according to your score on it.

Abide by the results of this test. If it shows that you really do need a basic course, take that course; but if it shows that you've got the necessary skills, pat yourself on the back for saving yourself some time and trouble.

To appeal your placement in a basic course, call your dean's office, explain the situation, and ask how you can take or retake the appropriate placement exam. At many schools, this may be as simple as calling up the appropriate office and scheduling a time to take the exam; at others, you may need the permission of someone in the testing office, your advisor, or your dean. Follow whatever directions the staff person in the dean's office gives you.

Solution 3: If you know a month or more before school begins that you will be expected to take a basic skills course, try to take this course that summer, before the academic year begins. If possible, take it at the college you'll be attending; if this isn't an option, take it at a different college near your home. (Sign up as a nondegree or extension student, so that you do not have to go through any formal application process; but *do* take the course for academic credit, so that you can transfer in those credits later.)

Most community colleges, junior colleges, and large universities offer these courses; those at community colleges and state universities are generally inexpensive.

If you get a C or higher in this basic class, you will then be ready to take regular classes in the fall. Let the registration office know that you have completed the basic course elsewhere, and make sure to have an official transcript sent as confirmation. You will then be eligible to register for regular instead of basic classes, and you should be able to transfer in your credits from the summer.

Solution 4: Even though you have been required or strongly encouraged to take a basic class, you may be able to get away with simply signing up for a higher-level class instead. Most registration computers are not programmed to catch people who register for more advanced classes than they are asked or required to take. If you are able to succeed in this higher-level class, then you'll receive credit for it and be able to continue.

However, this strategy is quite risky, and I recommend it only in cases where you feel quite sure that you have all the necessary basic skills. Most students who try this tactic quickly get weeded out of the higher-level classes and are sent back into basic skills courses. Others manage to start out decently enough, but find themselves sinking fast by the middle of the term.

Your school may strictly limit the number of credits you may complete in internships, volunteer work, and/or independent study.

Every college has different regulations on this. Some will allow you to do all the independent studies, internships, or volunteer work you want, but will let you apply only a limited number of credits for them toward your degree. Other schools will limit the number of such activities you may register for as a student.

Solution 1: Know the rules. Read the appropriate information in your college catalog carefully. If necessary, call your dean's office for details.

Solution 2: If you want to do an internship or volunteer work, but you've already earned the maximum number of credits allowable for such endeavors, try calling the internship or volunteer work an independent study instead. If you can find an instructor willing to sponsor such an independent study—and this isn't usually very difficult—then you can legitimately use those credits toward your degree (unless, of course, you've already completed the maximum number of independent study credits as well).

Your college may have strict limits on the number of credits or courses you may take on a pass-fail (or satisfactory-unsatisfactory) basis. It may also prohibit you from taking certain classes pass-fail.

Pass-fail grading is a wonderful invention: It enables you to study some difficult or unfamiliar subjects without running the risk of getting a low or mediocre grade. (You must of course do well enough in any pass-fail class to pass, however.)

At certain schools, all classes are graded pass-fail, and students receive detailed written evaluations instead of letter grades. In other schools, certain classes *must* be taken on a pass-fail basis. At most colleges, however, most or all courses are normally graded on the A through F system, though students may choose a pass-fail option for some or all of those courses instead if they wish.

If your school does offer you the pass-fail option, it may not permit you to take more than one class pass-fail per term. Other possible limitations: You may not take any courses in your major subject pass-fail; you may not take any pass-fail courses in your senior (or junior and senior) years; you may not take any upper-level courses pass-fail; you may apply only a certain number of credits earned in pass-fail toward your degree; certain classes may be taken only for letter grades.

Solution: Once again, know the rules. Read your college catalog carefully, or check with your dean's office. If you strongly believe that you merit an exception to a rule, make your case to the dean.

You may not be allowed to use a similar or even identical course taken at another college to fulfill a graduation requirement.

Earlier, on page 78, I explained how colleges can sometimes be fickle about transferring in credits from other schools. They can also be fickle about allowing you to use a course taken at another institution to satisfy a degree requirement.

This is a pretty common problem, but it's usually quite easy to solve—and to avoid.

Solution: If you've already taken some courses elsewhere and gotten them transferred in, go to see your dean after the transfer is complete. Bring with you a photocopy of your academic record, which you have obtained from your registration office. If you still have syllabi from any of the transfer courses you plan to discuss, photocopy them and bring these copies with you as well. Be polite and friendly throughout your meeting; keep in mind that you are not making a complaint, simply working out some details.

Show the dean your academic record, and explain exactly what graduation requirement(s) you wish to fulfill with which transfer course(s). Verbally outline the content of each transfer course; if you have copies of syllabi, show these to the dean as well.

The transfer course you wish to use to fulfill a graduation requirement does not have to be identical to the course that is normally required. So long as it covers some of the same material or is otherwise substantially similar, your dean may approve it. You can also usually get it approved if the course has a very similar title to the course normally required—even if the actual content of the two courses is very different.

Sometimes, however, two quite similar courses may have quite different titles. In such a case, it's important that you explain to your dean how similar the two courses are. As much as possible, give your dean a detailed rundown of what the transfer course included; a photocopied syllabus is especially helpful here.

In most cases, your dean will agree to any reasonable course substitution. Once he does agree, ask him to send a note to the registration office authorizing the substitution.

At some schools, decisions on substituting required courses with transfer classes are left up to the appropriate academic departments. This is fine; if your dean refers you to one or more departments, make your case before the department head(s).

In some cases you may be asked to provide written evidence to support your case—usually either a syllabus from the transfer course or a note from the teacher of the course describing its content. Such a request is perfectly legitimate, and these items are not usually hard to obtain. Simply call up the instructor, explain the situation, and ask for whatever you need. Follow up your request as necessary. If you are unable to reach the instructor, make your request of the secretary in the instructor's department office.

If you wish to have a course from another institution accepted in lieu of a course required for your *major or minor,* follow the same procedure described above—but bring your request to the appropriate department head instead of to your dean.

Lastly, if you plan to study at another institution in the future, and wish to use some of the credits you will earn there to satisfy your major, minor, or graduation requirements, check with your dean and/ or the appropriate department head at your college before you begin this study elsewhere. To avoid any potential complications, get the appropriate person's written approval before you leave campus—and make sure this written approval gets placed into your academic record.

Four years of full-time study may not be sufficient to earn a bachelor's degree. Two years of full-time study may not always be enough to earn an associate's degree.

Certain programs at some colleges require as much as five years (ten semesters or fifteen quarters) of full-time study in order to earn a bachelor's degree. Currently, ninety-five percent of these programs are in engineering and education; in the education programs, graduates simultaneously receive bachelor's degrees and teacher certification. Some states now require that all undergraduate teacher certification programs include five years of full-time study, or the equivalent; other states may soon adopt a similar requirement. However, quite a few colleges and universities continue to grant bachelor's degrees in engineering and/or education (including teacher certification) for four years (or less) of full-time study.

At some colleges, earning a bachelor's degree in *any* field in four academic years (eight semesters or twelve quarters) is extremely difficult, because they require as many as 128 semester credits or 192 quarter credits for graduation. This translates to a minimum of sixteen credits per term for four academic years. At these colleges, students typically take between four and five years of full-time study to complete their bachelor's degrees.

Some community and junior colleges also have high credit requirements; at these schools, students must complete at least sixteen credits per term for two full academic years to earn an associate's degree.

Solution 1: Know what you are getting into. When you begin researching colleges, read each catalog carefully. Find out how many credits you will need to graduate, and how many courses you will need to take each term in order to earn a bachelor's degree in four academic years (or an associate's degree in two). Three courses per term is reasonable, four tolerable, and five ridiculous.

If you are thinking about completing a program in engineering or teacher certification, examine each college's program carefully. Some schools may require a great deal more study (up to a full year more) than others.

As you do your research, you will see that at some colleges it is possible to earn bachelor's degrees (including engineering and education degrees) in only three or three and a half years of full-time study. You will also run across some five-year programs, including programs in education and engineering, that lead to both bachelor's and master's degrees.

Solution 2: Take classes in the summer. If you go to school year-round, you can reduce a five-year program to four years, and a four-year program to three. If your college does not offer classes in the summer, take classes elsewhere and transfer them in. Arrange in advance to have the summer courses accepted for transfer credit; see page 79 for details.

14

Housing and Food

On-campus housing and dining may be no bargain; in fact, either or both may be downright expensive.

Colleges vary enormously in what they charge for room and board. Rates range from about $2,700 per academic year to as much as $5,600 for room and board combined. Meals alone run from $1,400–$2,400 per academic year; housing alone typically runs from $1,600–$2,500, sometimes even higher for deluxe (by student standards) accommodations. Room and board costs at two different colleges can thus differ by as much as $2,500 or even $3,000 per year. For the extra money you may well be getting better food and housing—but you also may not be.

Some schools offer a range of housing options (shared triple room, shared double room, shared divided double, single room, shared four-person suite, etc.). Some colleges also offer one- or two-bedroom apartments for rent; often, though not always, these are available only to married students and students with children.

Usually these housing options are all priced differently. At some schools, however, all students pay the same room rate, whether they have private rooms or share doubles, triples, or suites.

Let's put the typical costs in perspective. At $2,700 (the minimum cost for room and board) per academic year, housing and dining run a total of $300 a month; at $5,600, the maximum, they run about $625 per month. That's $150 a week.

Solution 1: When shopping for a college, shop for room and board as well. Compare prices and quality.

Begin with prices. Most colleges list their housing and dining costs in their catalogs; if a college doesn't, call its housing office (or, if there is no such office, the student services or student affairs office) to get a current price quote. Financial aid may later reduce or eliminate your housing and dining costs—but it makes sense to know what the full price will be.

Then compare quality. When you visit campuses, make a point of eating at least two or three meals in college dining halls; if possible, eat in at least two different dining halls on each campus. If a college offers vegetarian, kosher, and/or co-op dining (see page 168 for details on co-ops), you may wish to sample these options as well.

Also on each campus visit, stay in a dorm overnight so that you can evaluate the accommodations. Are the building and room passably comfortable and reasonably quiet? What is the overall feel of the place? Can you imagine living there happily for nine months?

Visit as many other dorms as you can. In each one, look inside a typical room, at the common areas, and in at least one bathroom. Check for cleanliness, comfort, attractiveness, and the overall state of repair.

Remember that dorms can range from comfortable to unappealing to prisonlike, not only from one school to the next, but on a single campus. Many schools, for example, have converted gorgeous old mansions into very pleasant dorms; some of these same schools have also built newer, ugly, industrial-looking (and industrial-feeling) housing complexes.

Solution 2: Eat and/or live off campus. At many colleges, an off-campus apartment shared with one to three other students will be cheaper per person than sharing a double room on campus—plus, you each get your own room. Renting a room in someone's home is also frequently cheaper than a shared dorm room. With the cost of on-campus board averaging about sixty-five dollars per week, you may well be able to save money (though not time) by doing your own cooking, too, or sharing the cooking with your roommates. Cooking on your own also allows you to pick what, when, and where you eat.

Doing your own cooking is nowhere near as difficult as it may appear at first. In fact, there are several cookbooks especially for college students which will teach you all the basics and give you many quick, simple, inexpensive recipes. One such popular book is *The*

College Cookbook by Geri Harrington (Storey Communications, 1988).

Solution 3: Eat and/or live in a co-op. Many colleges now offer this option, in which dining halls and/or dorms are run by students themselves. Housing co-op members must share in the effort of cleaning and maintaining the building; members of a dining co-op share in the tasks of preparing, serving, and cleaning up after meals. Co-ops usually cost ten to twenty percent less than regular college room and board. Co-ops usually have a sense of community and camaraderie, and co-op food is usually tastier than the standard college fare.

In many college towns there are also a number of private co-ops— group houses that are privately owned, but where all residents share in the preparation of meals and the cleaning and maintenance of the building. These co-op houses sometimes have vacancies, especially during summers and at the beginning of each term; vacancies are often advertised on campus bulletin boards and/or in the student newspaper.

Some colleges will require you to live in dorms and/or eat in college dining halls, whether you want to or not.

Many colleges and universities require most or all students to live and eat on campus during their freshman year. Some extend that requirement through the sophomore year. A few colleges, mostly small liberal arts schools, require even juniors and seniors to live and/ or eat in campus facilities.

Often there's some educational theory behind this. At certain liberal arts schools, for example, the on-campus housing or dining requirement is intended to help foster and strengthen a sense of community among students.

At other schools, the rationale is very different: Students (usually freshmen) are assumed to be too irresponsible and unskilled to be able to live safely or productively on their own. They are thus kept on campus, where they can be more closely supervised and controlled.

Still other colleges require students to live or eat on campus for strictly financial reasons: Back in the 1940s and 1950s, when virtually all students wanted desperately to live in dorms and eat in dining halls, many schools invested millions in building the facilities to accommodate them. Now those colleges are stuck with these expensive buildings, which they must either use, close, or convert into offices or classrooms. Many schools choose to keep these facilities open by requiring some, most, or all students to eat and/or live in them.

Solution: Before you apply to any college—or at least before you accept admission—find out what the regulations are for eating and living on campus. These usually appear in college catalogs; complete and up-to-date details are available from the office(s) of housing and dining, or from the admissions office.

If the housing or dining rules at a college seem too strict, be sure to ask if there are any exceptions to them. Many colleges exempt some or all of the following people from on-campus housing or dining requirements: married students; students with children; students with physical disabilities; students over the age of twenty-two or twenty-three; part-time students; students with special dietary needs; and students who live with their parents within ten or fifteen miles of the college.

Some colleges may permit you to live and/or eat off campus, but will charge you a fee to do so.

Although it is rare, a few colleges (mostly liberal arts schools) that require many or most of their students to live or dine on campus charge those who do not do so a fee each term for the privilege. The fee goes to help maintain the dorms and dining halls, and usually runs between fifty and three hundred dollars per term.

Solution: If a college does require some of its students to eat or live on campus, check with the housing and dining office(s) to find out whether students who live or eat elsewhere are charged such a fee, and how much that fee currently runs. Be sure to factor in this cost when deciding where to live and where to eat.

At some schools, you will need to request a dorm room four or more months in advance to be sure of getting one.

Although some colleges have to force students to live on campus in order to fill all their dorms, at other schools dorm space is at a premium. At some colleges and universities, all dorm rooms for the fall may be spoken for by the end of May, or even earlier.

Solution: As soon as you have made your decision which college's offer of admission to accept, let the admissions office know. If you wish to live on campus, *call* the college's housing office that same day and ask how to reserve a dorm room. Follow the instructions you receive as promptly as possible.

This is yet another reason to apply to colleges early. The earlier you apply, the earlier (in most cases) you'll be offered admission or rejected; and the sooner you're offered admission, the sooner you can accept it and apply for a dorm room.

If, for whatever reason, all dorms are full at the time you apply for a room, ask to be placed on the waiting list. Every college that offers on-campus housing keeps such a list. Dorm rooms do open up as the weeks pass and students opt out of on-campus housing (or out of attending the college entirely).

Some colleges overcrowd their dorms, putting three or even four students in rooms made for two. Colleges have even been known to house students in alcoves, basements, and other normally nonresidential spaces.

No college deliberately plans on overcrowding its students. However, many colleges routinely overbook their dorm spaces, just as airlines overbook their flights, on the assumption that some students won't show at the beginning of the term or school year. Although the people in each college's housing office know from experience about how many students will be no-shows, sometimes more students show up than expected—and the school suddenly finds itself with more students than it can accommodate. Usually this situation occurs only during the fall term.

Most colleges deal with this situation by temporarily putting a third student in a double room, a fifth in a four-person suite, etc. On occasion, schools have even turned basements, offices, and other storage spots into temporary housing for students.

Any such arrangement is always intended as a strictly temporary measure. The assumption is that as students drop out during the term or at the term's end, people can be reshuffled into normal, bearable rooming arrangements.

With virtually no exceptions, by the end of the term things do get straightened out—but they may or may not get straightened out any sooner. You might have to endure overcrowding just for the first few days of the term—or you might have to live with it through the term's end.

Solution 1: When you apply for housing, request a single room. Colleges are more likely to place an extra person in a room already meant for two or more people than they are to put a second person in a room meant for one.

Solution 2: If you do find yourself in overcrowded conditions, you should have the right to move off campus if you wish and receive a full refund of both the room rental charge and your room deposit. You should have this right if your room is overcrowded *even* if your college would normally require you to live on campus.

A college cannot have things both ways: It cannot tell you that you must live on campus *and* that it does not have sufficient space to reasonably house you.

You and your parents should both contact the college's housing office as soon as you find out about the overcrowding. Explain the situation, and insist on either being given normal (e.g., two people to a double room, etc.) on-campus accommodations or being permitted to live off campus and having all dorm costs refunded. With few exceptions, one of these two options will be granted.

Solution 3: Accept the very cramped conditions but insist on getting some of your money back. If, for example, you've paid the full cost of sharing a double room with one other person, but when you get to college you find that there are two other people in that double room with you, you should be entitled to a refund of some of your money. You and your parents should both contact the college's housing office and insist that you be given either normal accommodations or a partial refund.

Solution 4: If the housing office will not get the extra person out of your room, will not allow you to move off campus, *and* cannot find you more reasonable quarters, it's time to file a complaint. You and your parents should both contact the dean in charge of housing, and insist that she satisfactorily resolve the situation. This dean will have the title of dean of housing, dean of housing and dining, dean of student services, dean of student life, or dean of student affairs.

Many dorm rooms are tiny, ugly, and inhospitable.

Some schools have some pretty awful dormitories. But even those with awful dorms usually have at least a few habitable ones as well.

Solution: When you make your campus visits, check out as many dorms as possible—all of them, if you can. Then, when you apply for a dorm rooms, *request housing in a specific dorm.* Better yet, pick the three dorms that most appeal to you and request them as your first, second, and third choices.

If the housing application form does not have a space for choosing a specific dorm, choose one or more anyway. Staple a separate note to the top of the form (don't use a paper clip; if you do, the note may get separated and ignored). Most people in housing offices will try to give you one of the dorms you request if they can.

In some dorms, certain types of rooms (singles, doubles, suites, etc.) are more hospitable than others. Feel free to also request a single room, a suite, or whatever type of room you prefer. Or, rank your first three choices.

Many dorms are dirty and/or in disrepair.

Solution 1: Same as above.

Solution 2: If something needs repair, let the maintenance people know about it. See page 180 for details on getting things fixed.

Your dorm may be noisy, especially late at night and on weekends.

Many students stay up late, and many play loud music well into the night. Dorms are particularly likely to be noisy and filled with partying on Friday and Saturday nights.

Solution 1: If noise bothers you, clearly state in your housing application that you wish to live in a quiet dorm. If there is no special place to indicate this on your application, write a separate note and staple it to the application.

Some colleges specifically designate certain dorms as quiet dorms. These have fairly strict regulations on noise. However, even if your college has no official quiet dorms, the housing staff may still do their best to put students who ask for quiet living quarters together in the same dorms or on the same floors.

Solution 2: Buy earplugs. For a dollar or two at any drugstore you can get comfortable, safe earplugs that significantly reduce outside noise. *These really work.*

The choice is yours: You can privately curse your noisy neighbors, you can confront them and ask them to quiet down, or you can pop in your earplugs and solve your problem in an instant.

Solution 3: Live in quiet quarters off campus.

You may be given a roommate who has very different habits than you, who is difficult to get along with, or who is an outright twit.

Some colleges assign roommates at random. Many, however, will do at least a modest amount of matchmaking. Typically they'll put people together based on one or two significant personal details such as religion, race, main interests, etc.

Still, whatever method housing offices use, roommate assignments are always a crapshoot. You might wind up with the ideal roommate—or you might wind up with the Roommate from Hell.

Solution 1: Most college's housing applications include a few personal questions, the answers to which will help the people in housing match you up with a compatible roommate. Consider these questions carefully, and answer them thoroughly and honestly. Add any other information that you think might be important—for example, "I'm crazy about football," "I'm a very early riser," "I'm deeply involved in the Catholic church," etc. Also feel free to state what you would like in a roommate—for instance, "I'd love to room with another musician," "I would prefer to share a room with another person of color," "Please give me a roommate who's quiet," and so on.

If your housing application doesn't ask about you or about what you want in a roommate, take the initiative and volunteer this information. Write it on a separate sheet and staple it to your application. The more specific information the housing staff have, the more likely they are to match you up with a roommate you'll appreciate—or at least get along with.

Solution 2: If you don't like or get along with the roommate(s) you've been assigned, switch rooms. This can be done either officially or unofficially.

The official way is to tell the housing office that you and your roommate are incompatible, and that you'd like to be moved to a different room. (Don't ask to have your roommate moved; it won't work. Just speak for yourself.) Sometimes this works and sometimes it doesn't; a lot depends on what other spaces are available and how accommodating the housing people are.

Sometimes it helps if you and your roommate go to the housing office together and both request new roommates. If the housing staff people know that both of you are unhappy with each other, they may be more likely to reassign one of you to another room.

One way to dramatically increase your chances of making an official roommate change is to find someone you like who is willing to room with you. The two of you can then make a joint request to room with one another. Another option is to find someone to do a switch with: You agree to move in with her roommate, and she agrees to move in with yours. Housing staff people are usually quite willing to go along with either such arrangement.

Switching rooms or roommates unofficially is much easier: You simply arrange everything yourself, without letting any of the people in the housing office know. This strategy has some drawbacks, however. As far as the folks in the housing office are concerned, you still live with your original roommate in your original dorm room. Thus you are still responsible for what happens to that room; if it is damaged through neglect or abuse, you're the one who may have to pay for the damage. Unofficial room changes may also cause some confusion with mail delivery or telephone calls.

One solution that usually works is to make an unofficial room or roommate switch first; then let the people in the housing office know about it, and ask them to make it official. Usually they'll be perfectly agreeable, though occasionally a housing staff person may throw a fit, lecture you about the sin of unauthorized room reassignment, and insist that everyone go back to the very roommates they so carefully arranged to avoid.

Solution 3: You can often avoid the whole roommate crapshoot altogether by requesting a specific person as your roommate. Better yet, the two of you can request each other.

If you know someone else who will be attending the same college, and the two of you want to share a room, each of you should write on your housing application (or in a letter attached to your application), "I wish to room with _____, whose social security number is _____." The great majority of these requests are routinely approved.

You may not be permitted to stay in your dorm room during vacations, even those of only one week. A few colleges even prohibit students from staying in dorms over Thanksgiving vacation.

At most schools, you must be out of your dorm room shortly after the last day of exams (at a few colleges, *on* the last day of exams). At most colleges, you also may not stay in the dorm during spring break, Christmas break, and other breaks.

Solution: Find out from the housing office early in the school year exactly what your college's policy is regarding staying in or vacating dorms during vacations. Also find out if there are any exceptions; for example, if you are a foreign student, you may be permitted to stay in your dorm during certain vacations even though most students are not.

If you must go elsewhere during breaks, and are unwilling or unable to go home, ask some of your friends if you can stay with them and their families. A great number of students stay with friends' families during breaks, and plenty of families are happy to serve as hosts.

Off-campus housing may be difficult to find. What is available may be expensive, ugly, and/or poorly maintained.

Off-campus housing varies tremendously from place to place. In some small college and university towns, there is a tremendous demand for off-campus housing; as a result, rooms and apartments are hard to come by, landlords have little incentive to maintain their properties well, and rents are high. In other college towns, however, the housing supply has risen to meet the demand, so lots of rooms and apartments are available at affordable prices. In most big cities, there is a huge range of housing options to choose from, though sometimes rooms and apartments near campus are at a premium.

In general, rooms and apartments intended for rental to students are not maintained as well or repaired as quickly as other rental properties, for these reasons: (1) most students have lower standards and expectations for housing than other people; (2) students generally demand fewer repairs and make fewer complaints; (3) students tend to inflict a great deal of wear and tear on rooms and apartments; and

(4) landlords can usually get away with poor maintenance and few repairs.

Solution 1: Begin looking for housing early. For fall off-campus housing, start looking and asking around a month before the end of the spring term. For housing for other terms, begin your search two months before the term begins.

Places to look for information on rooms and apartments for rent:

● The classified ads of your campus newspaper.

● The classified ads of the town or city newspaper. Although some ads for rentals appear every day, the great majority of them run only in the Sunday (or, in some cities and towns, the Saturday) paper, in the big weekly real estate section.

● Other publications: neighborhood newspapers, weekly advertising papers, etc.

● Campus bulletin boards, particularly those in the student center.

● The college housing office. Many housing offices have a file, book, or bulletin board listing off-campus rentals. Typically, however, these listings are not updated as frequently as they should be, so forty to seventy-five percent of the rooms or apartments you call about may already be rented.

● Bulletin boards at neighborhood grocery stores, Laundromats, drugstores, convenience stores, churches, and other organizations and businesses.

● Front yards. Cruise the town or neighborhood where you want to live, looking for "for rent" signs in windows and on lawns.

Solution 2: Talk to people. Ask your friends, acquaintances, classmates, and teachers if they know of a room or apartment that will (or might) become available. Follow up any leads.

One of the very best ways to find decent housing is to find out which of your friends currently live off campus. Visit them in their rooms or apartments during the term, and make note of which places you might like to live in. Five or six weeks before the end of the term, ask them, "Are you planning to live in the same place next term [or next year]?" If they aren't, tell them that you're interested in renting the space once they've moved out. Ask them for their landlord's name and phone number, and call the landlord promptly. Many good places to live pass from student to student in this manner, without ever being advertised.

It is also a good idea to ask people about their landlords. Are they reasonable and fair? Do they make major repairs fairly quickly? What about minor repairs? Are they easy to get along with? *Avoid bizarre or unreasonable landlords at all times,* no matter how nice their rooms or apartments might be; these people will only make your life miserable, and you'll end up having to move in the middle of the term.

Solution 3: The farther you live from campus, the less competition there will be for rental housing—and, usually, the more choice you will have, the lower rents will tend to be, and the better maintained the properties will often be. The neighborhood may be quieter, too. If finding housing is a problem, or if you want a nicer home or neighborhood, look in neighborhoods and towns that are a few miles away from campus.

If you have a car, living some miles from campus is rarely a problem. However, don't dismiss this option even if you don't have a car. Check the campus and/or city bus services to see where and when buses run. Consider biking to and from campus. Take into account your schedule, your available time, safety, and cost.

Solution 4: Be choosy. If where and how you live are important to you, don't settle for a place you'll be unhappy in. Remember, whatever room or apartment you rent, you're going to have to spend at least a term there; why not live in a place you like? Be willing to look at (and, if need be, turn down) five or even ten places in order to find one that you'll be comfortable in. If need be, let a barely passable place slip through your fingers in order to find one that's more to your liking.

Sometimes finding a decent place can take a while, especially in student neighborhoods. *Don't* believe landlords, friends, or anyone else who says, "All the student spaces are the same; there aren't any nice [or nicer] ones available." The great majority of the time, this simply isn't true; you just have to look long or hard enough.

Solution 5: Remember that wherever you live, you will not be sitting in an empty room, staring at bare walls. Pick a place not only because of how it looks now, but because of what you can do with it. Imagine each space with a little furniture in it, and some posters on the walls, and perhaps a few plants.

Solution 6: Be an assertive (but not a demanding) tenant. If you see a place you like but that has *one or two* things that need fixing, tell the landlord directly, "I like what I see, and I'll take the place if you'll take care of _____ and _____ before I move in." If the landlord says no, you probably should keep looking elsewhere.

If the landlord agrees to fix the problems, but they are still there when you move in, call the landlord immediately. Calmly, politely, but firmly let him know that you expect the problems to be fixed promptly.

The food in the dining hall may be abominable, and it will likely be heavy on starch.

Ideally, you sampled the food in at least a couple of dining halls at each college when you made your campus visits, and you took food into consideration when deciding which college to attend.

However, no college has truly excellent food, and at most schools the food ranges from mediocre to poor. Starches tend to prevail, and on bad days the food may be downright inedible.

Solution 1: If your college offers more than one meal plan, consider all your options carefully. Many colleges offer vegetarian and/or kosher meal plans as well as a standard plan, and both of these alternatives almost always have better food. Plenty of students who are neither vegetarians nor Jewish opt for these plans, simply because they offer tastier fare.

Solution 2: Eat in a dining co-op. Co-op food is usually better-tasting and more varied than what regular college dining halls offer. Co-op dining tends to cost ten to twenty percent less per term, too.

Solution 3: Eat on a limited-meal plan. Many colleges will allow you to eat just suppers, or just lunches and suppers, in college dining halls, at a significantly reduced rate. The rest of the time you are free to eat elsewhere or cook for yourself. Some limited-meal plans also do not include Sunday suppers or any weekend meals.

A fair number of schools also have pay-as-you-go plans, where you can eat in campus dining halls as often or an infrequently as you like.

Solution 4: Cook for yourself. Cooking is a very valuable skill, and it's really not hard to learn. Furthermore, if you eat on your own, you get to enjoy the foods you want at the time you want to eat. For more details on cooking for yourself, see pages 167–168.

Some colleges offer no on-campus dining or housing at all.

Community, vocational, technical, and most junior colleges offer no housing, and usually no on-campus dining except perhaps tiny pay-as-you-go cafeterias. The food in these cafeterias is usually atrocious. Most business colleges offer no housing or dining of any kind.

Solution: Pack a lunch or a supper, or pick one up on the way to class.

You will probably put on weight at college, particularly during your freshman year.

I'm speaking statistically here. It is not your inevitable destiny to gain weight once you get to college; indeed, you may well end up losing it. But most students put on about fifteen pounds (known as the "freshman fifteen") during their first year of college. In part, this simply occurs because people's bodies mature and fill in; but it also happens because college food tends to be starchy and high-calorie, and because students often eat lots of junk food and drink a fair amount of alcohol.

Solution: If you're concerned about gaining weight, follow these tried-and-true techniques for taking and keeping weight off:

Exercise regularly. When you can, walk or bicycle instead of driving or riding.

Limit the amount of sugar and starch you eat. Drink diet soft drinks instead of regular ones.

Drink alcohol in moderation.

When you start to put weight on, cut out sugar and/or alcohol until you drop back to your normal weight.

15

Campus Facilities

College maintenance people will not always be quick to fix or replace things that are broken. In some cases they may never fix them at all.

Large numbers of students—and individual students who are careless, thoughtless, or outright destructive—create a great deal of wear and tear on buildings, furniture, streets, sidewalks, and just about everything else. Much of this wear and tear never gets taken care of because it never gets reported.

Solution: If something is broken, missing, or otherwise in need of attention, *report it.* Two problems out of three don't get taken care of because most students are too unconcerned, uninformed, or lazy to tell the proper people about it.

The office to report such problems to is called either maintenance or buildings and grounds. You'll be amazed at how helpful and responsive the people in this office can be—if only you'll let them know what needs to be done.

Normally a polite phone call is all that it takes. At some schools, however, you may be asked to come down to the office to fill out a work order. If you *are* asked to fill out one of these, do so; college policy may require the maintenance people to get a written work order before fixing anything.

If something remains unrepaired after a reasonable amount of time has passed, make a follow-up call. If necessary, call a third time. In the unlikely event that call number three doesn't bring results, contact the dean of student affairs. Explain what the problem is, what you have done to try to get it corrected, and what has and has not happened so far. The dean should be willing and able to take care of the problem for you.

There may not be enough of some items or services to go around. Microcomputer labs may not have enough computers; math or writing labs may be understaffed; some facilities, especially the library, may not be open enough hours.

Solution 1: When services and facilities are stretched thin, the key to getting the most out of them is timing. At the beginning of each term, find out the hours of any labs, centers, or other facilities that you expect to use on a regular basis. Also find out if it is possible to reserve time or make appointments at any of these; if it is, make appointments or reservations anywhere that they are accepted.

If reserving a time or a spot isn't possible, try to use the facilities during the hours when they are in least demand: in the morning, late at night, and during mealtimes.

Solution 2: If your college has too little of something, write or call the provost and let her know. Explain exactly what seems to be lacking, how you can tell that it's lacking (you always have to wait in line, you can never get an appointment, it's never open when you can get there, etc.), and what you think is needed (more computers, longer hours, etc.). Be polite but concerned, and ask her for her help.

Your letter or call alone may not make much of a difference, but it will at least alert the provost—and, thus, the college administration—to the problem. And if the provost gets several other calls and letters as well, she may be convinced to make some changes.

Some colleges have few or no athletic facilities.

Most business, vocational, and technical colleges provide little or nothing in the way of athletic facilities. Very small liberal arts colleges (those with eight hundred or fewer students) and junior colleges also tend to have few or no facilities.

Solution: If athletics are important to you, ask each admissions officer about the athletic facilities at his school before you apply. In some cases, you may simply have to join the Y or a health club.

Small colleges (those with fewer than two thousand students) often have inadequate libraries. Most community and junior colleges also have very small libraries. Most business, vocational, and technical colleges have no libraries at all.

As a rule, large universities have good libraries; large liberal arts colleges have passable ones; and other schools have poor ones.

Solution 1: Make use of the other college and public libraries in the area. Get a local library card; ask if other colleges' libraries will let you take out books and magazines on your student ID (sometimes they will).

Solution 2: Use interlibrary loan. It's either free or very inexpensive (twenty-five cents to a dollar per book or periodical), and you can sit back while the people in the library do all the work of finding things for you. Items usually take two to six weeks to arrive, so plan ahead.

Solution 3: Some college and public libraries have access to a computerized data base which lists all the books, magazines, and other items in every library in the city, county, or metropolitan area. This data base can help you locate materials quickly and easily. Ask the staff at the libraries in your area if they have such a data base on-line.

Solution 4: If there is a book or journal that you expect to use quite often but that your college library does not have, talk to an acquisitions librarian about it. Politely explain what you need, why you need it, and, if possible, why other students may need it as well; then ask if he'll order it for the library. You'll be amazed at how often you'll be told, "Okay, I'll order it soon."

You may be unfairly fined for library books you already returned.

Nearly every student runs into this problem. The main cause seems to be optical scanners that fail to register an item's return.

Solution: As much as possible, avoid using book drops. Return books and other materials in person; watch and wait while each item is run past the optical scanner. *Then ask the librarian to call up your name on her computer and see if you still have any items checked out.*

If the scanner has missed an item, it will be listed as still being checked out. You can nip the problem in the bud right here by saying, "Wait a minute—I just returned that right now. There it is right in front of you."

Once more, watch and wait while the item is run past the scanner. Then have the librarian call up your name a second time to make sure the item's return has registered on the computer.

But don't walk away yet. As a backup, request a receipt showing all of the call numbers of the items you returned *and* the date you returned them; this receipt *must* be filled out *in ink* and signed or initialed by a librarian (also in ink).

Most college libraries have official receipts which are available on request; if your library doesn't have them, a plain piece of paper is fine. To save time, get a handful of receipts at the beginning of each term; fill one out in ink each time you have materials to return, and simply have a librarian sign and date it.

Should you be unjustly accused of not returning a book or some other library item, simply show the librarian your receipt.

Most colleges have too few photocopying machines, particularly in their libraries.

The copying machines in college libraries often seem to have lines of people waiting to use them; on occasion, so do machines elsewhere on campus. Ten to twenty percent of the copiers are typically out of order at any given time, making the situation worse.

Solution 1: Early in your first term on campus—or, if possible, before the term begins—scope out all the on-campus copiers.

Start with the library. Ask a librarian for the location of every photocopier in the entire library; then pay a visit to each one. Usually at least one or two will be in an out-of-the-way, relatively untraveled part of the library. These are the copiers to head for whenever you need to make copies in the library. (If your school has more than one library, check out the photocopiers in each library you are likely to use.)

Then do the same for the student union. Ask at the union information desk for the location of all the copiers in the building.

Next visit the campus duplicating center. Find out its prices and hours; then ask the staff person there where else on campus photocopiers can be found. Check these out as well.

By the time you are done, you will have a mental map of all the photocopiers on campus. By the third or fourth week of the term, you will also have a good idea which machines are most likely to be available.

Solution 2: As much as possible, do your photocopying during the least busy hours: in the morning, late at night, and during meals.

Solution 3: Go to an off-campus copy shop. These are often strategically situated near or just off campus. Some are open late into the night, or even twenty-four hours a day. Check the Yellow Pages under "Copying" or "Photocopying" for the nearest locations.

Also scout out the immediate neighborhood for copying machines at nearby banks, print shops, grocery stores, drugstores, public libraries, etc.

College campuses are not always safe—and not always adequately patrolled by police.

Most college campuses are safer than the cities, suburbs, or towns that surround them. However, crime remains a problem on virtually all college campuses, particularly at night. The higher the crime in the surrounding area, the more watchful you need to be, both on and off campus.

The majority of colleges have improved their security in recent years. Many have added emergency telephones, more police protection, and/or evening escort services. However, your best defense against crime is still your own watchfulness and alertness.

Solution 1: When you leave your dorm room, even for just a few minutes, close and lock your door. An open door is an invitation for thieves.

A major portion of on-campus crime is committed by students. It's easy to slip into an unlocked room down the hall, grab a purse or wallet, and slip out again. Discourage thieves from both on and off campus by keeping your door locked.

Other tips on avoiding theft:

• Keep your purse with you. Don't leave it under a seat, on a coatrack, or in your car while you run to the bathroom.

• Lock your car whenever and wherever you park it. Don't leave tempting items (your briefcase, tapes, etc.) in full view.

• Always lock your bike with a strong bicycle lock whenever and wherever you park it. If your front wheel is removable, take it off and lock it up as well. Bicycle theft is one of the most common campus crimes.

• If possible, check or lock up your belongings when you go into the campus bookstore—or take them in with you. Simply leaving your things on an open shelf invites theft.

Solution 2: If you're a woman, avoid walking alone at night, especially after 11:00 P.M. When possible, walk in groups of three or more. When alone, make use of campus shuttle buses and/or the evening escort service. Escort services are free, and usually efficient and reliable. Call the campus police or campus operator for the phone number.

I also recommend carrying a loud whistle in your purse or pocket at all times. Blow the whistle loudly whenever you're in trouble. This simple act will discourage many criminals and summon help quickly. You can get a good, inexpensive whistle at any sporting goods store, and at many drug or discount stores.

If you live or go to school in a tough neighborhood, you may also want to carry a small can of Mace with you for added self-defense. Mace is available at gun shops.

Solution 3: Most schools sponsor at least one self-protection and crime-prevention workshop each term. If your school offers one, take it. Call your campus police or the office of student affairs to find out if, when, and where one will be offered.

Solution 4: If your school has an emergency phone system, learn the location of every phone. Emergency phones should be noted on any college map; if they aren't, call the campus police for locations.

If you frequently work late at night in the same place, it is also a good idea to note where the nearest accessible regular phone is located.

Campus buildings at a great many colleges are still not wheelchair-accessible.

If you use a wheelchair, you want to be able to get into every building and, ideally, every room on campus. Unfortunately, this is not yet possible at most colleges.

Solution: Before you enroll in any college—and, preferably, before you even apply—find out exactly which buildings and floors are wheelchair-accessible and which ones are not.

Most colleges have an office called handicapped services, special services, or disability services—or at least a staffer in the student services office who serves as an advocate for students with disabilities. Give this office or person a call and ask about on-campus access for wheelchairs. Also ask to be sent a map of the campus on which all wheelchair-accessible buildings and all handicapped parking spots have been marked. Make sure this map has a comprehensive key, so that you can tell which buildings contain classrooms, which contain labs, which are dorms, and so on.

As I discussed in chapter 1, before enrolling (and, ideally, applying) anywhere, try to visit the colleges that most interest you. Campus visits will give you a clear and complete sense of which areas are accessible and which ones are not.

16

Other Students

Not all college students are intelligent, or even mentally awake.

You don't need a great deal in the way of brains to get into most colleges. Many schools require nothing more than a C average in high school; others just ask for a high school diploma or GED; and a great many others do not require even this.

But even the colleges that carefully select their students don't always enroll the most intelligent people. At many high schools, it's quite possible to earn high grades without doing any real thinking; what may really count are the ability to memorize and a willingness to do whatever you're told. Many students are thus able to earn high grades in high school and get into selective colleges on the basis of those grades, even though there's not a great deal actually going on inside their heads. I've met straight-A students who have never asked an important question or had an original idea in their entire lives.

Solution: Choose your friends carefully. When you first meet people, make no assumptions about their knowledge, wisdom, or ability to think and question. Avoid relying on first impressions unless they are overwhelmingly obvious. Observe people carefully as the days and weeks pass, and let them demonstrate to you through their speech and actions how (and if) they think.

This advice also applies well to teachers, administrators, future bosses, and just about everyone else you will encounter in life.

Some of your fellow students will be fools, braggarts, manipulators, bores, thieves, narcissists, greedheads, or all-around jerks. Some will act exactly as they did in high school.

Replace the word "students" in the above paragraph with "human beings," and you've got a true statement about our entire species.

Solution: Avoid these people. They have little or nothing to offer you, and they will make your own life less rewarding and more difficult. All of them, at base, are selfish and uncaring.

When you meet new people, particularly people in whom you see a possible romantic interest, be friendly but wary. Build friendships and romantic relationships slowly and carefully; let people prove themselves worthy of your attention, friendship, or love first.

Some of the students in your dorm or classes will belong to organizations such as the Irish Republican Army, the Hare Krishnas, Jehovah's Witnesses, the Jewish Defense League, Nichiren Shoshu, or Scientology. These folks may pressure you to join their groups, or at least attend a propaganda session.

With few exceptions, colleges are small melting pots. At most schools, students represent nearly every possible religious, political, and social belief or organization. Lots of people in these groups are sincere believers, and many of them are very decent human beings; some members' ethics and/or mental stability, however, are highly questionable.

While you're in college, chances are good that members of many of these groups will attempt to persuade, coax, or coerce you into attending a group meeting. Usually they will be willing to keep pushing, cajoling, urging, and bothering you until you finally give in.

Solution: If you listen politely to one of these people, try to hold a conversation with him, or try to debate him, he will simply continue to pressure you until you give in.

So don't listen politely or try to talk with him. Instead, as soon as you get wind of his intention, look him straight in the eye and say firmly—interrupting him if necessary—"Thank you, but I'm not interested." Then walk away.

He may pursue you, attempt to continue the conversation, ask you a leading question, or even insult you to try to recapture your attention. *Continue walking away;* if need be, turn to him again and say, *extremely* firmly, "I said I'm not interested. Please go away."

If he *still* persists, lock your eyes on his and say grimly, "Fuck off." Walk away quickly; ignore whatever abuse he may then heap upon you.

If someone tries to apply pressure to you over the phone, say, "I'm not interested, thank you; please don't call back," and immediately hang up. If the person keeps talking to try to keep you on the phone—and they probably will—say firmly, "Good-bye," interrupting him if necessary, and hang up.

Of course, if you *are* genuinely interested in visiting one or more of these groups, or in talking with a group member about his (or your) beliefs, feel free to.

Some of your fellow students will constantly try to sound and act intellectual, and will pretend that academia is everything. These people are likely to also act (and feel) superior, and they may insult you or put you down, in or out of class.

These poor people usually do not even realize that they are merely playing a role. They also don't realize how foolish they look to most students—and to most teachers.

Furthermore, they don't realize that most *real* scholars and teachers, the ones who contribute something worthwhile to the world, usually speak in plain English, and normally lead full lives outside of academia.

Instructors respond to these pretentious students in three ways. Some are perfectly polite and helpful to them, but privately think of them as dorks. Some (usually the poorest instructors) appreciate the airs these students put on and reward them for it, sometimes by adopting them as teacher's pets. Many instructors, however, are completely unmoved by these students either way.

It is an unfortunate fact that many of these students become honor students.

Solution: Ignore these pathetic folks. Get on with your life.

If one of these people baits you in class, don't rise to the bait; that's exactly what she wants. If she tries to get a reaction out of you by insulting you or your work, by spreading rumors about you, or by refusing to even speak with you, refuse to show your anger. Don't argue with her, debate her, or try to win her favor. And, most of all, don't try to copy her. Simply be who you are, do your best work, and make no apologies for either yourself or your work. If somehow you threaten or offend her, that's her problem.

Although they may not appear so on the surface, such students are actually terribly frightened, insecure, and unhappy.

Some students will try to suck up to teachers by flattering them, parroting them, or batting their eyelashes at them.

Most good teachers despise this ass-licking behavior, though most will be too polite to say anything about it in class. Some teachers, however—usually the least interesting and competent ones—can't get enough of it.

Solution: Pick the best teachers you can. When someone starts brownnosing an instructor in class, either ignore it or look at the teacher and roll your eyes a bit.

Under no circumstances should you suck up to teachers yourself. Of course, if you like a teacher, feel free to talk with him, work closely with him, or become friends with him. But don't falsely flatter him. It's sleazy, it undermines any genuine relationship between you and your teacher, and more often than not it backfires.

Some students may ask you to let them copy your papers or otherwise help them to cheat.

Many college students occasionally consider cheating, and at least twenty-five percent of them do cheat or plagiarize at least once. Of these, a significant portion get caught, because college instructors, unlike high school teachers, are very good at spotting fraud.

If you knowingly let someone else copy your work and he gets caught, chances are excellent that you will be held equally accountable. You will probably be given an F in the class as punishment, and you may also be suspended or expelled from the college.

Nevertheless, in some student circles cheating is considered normal, and you may be strongly pressured to participate. You may even be criticized for refusing to do so.

Solution: No matter what goes on around you, *do not* cheat on exams, plagiarize papers, or allow others to cheat or plagiarize from your own work. It's clearly unethical, and it simply isn't worth the risk: The chances of getting caught (or of the person who copies your work getting caught) are too great.

If another student whom you do not already know well sells you drugs, you may get burned—or, worse, arrested.

I neither recommend nor approve of the use of illegal drugs. On the other hand, it's a simple fact that lots of college students use them, particularly marijuana. It's also a fact that in our culture's current antidrug frenzy, we are trying to stomp out the problem by punishing drug users, sometimes severely.

Drug dealing is not an honest business. The tighter the current crackdown on illegal drug use gets, the more dishonest the business will become. What you pay for may thus not be what you get.

Furthermore, our law enforcement people have learned that one of the most effective ways to locate and arrest drug users is to have undercover agents pose as dealers. *Therefore, any person who wishes to sell you drugs whom you do not already know as a friend, relative, or reasonably close acquaintance may be a policeman.*

Solution: If you choose to use illegal drugs, be extremely discreet about where you use them and extremely careful whom you buy them from. Don't make a purchase from anyone unless you already know and trust him.

Remember, too, that our culture is currently unable to distinguish between relatively benign drugs such as marijuana and truly dangerous ones such as crack, ice, crank, and heroin. What may seem— and be—just an ounce of pot to you may look to police and judges like the Evil Weed from Hell. If you smoke marijuana, keep both the pot and your use of it carefully hidden.

Important: If you believe that you may have become dependent upon any drug, or if a problem arises as a result of your drug use, *don't* be discreet about your need for help. Seek counseling promptly. Call First Call for Help and ask for the phone number of the local drug emergency hotline. If there is no First Call for Help in your town, ask the directory assistance operator. Your college may also have its own drug or emergency hotline; call the college operator for the extension number.

A great many college students don't use contraception; many don't even think about it.

A large percentage of otherwise intelligent college students either are ignorant of basic birth control methods or don't have the foresight or patience to use them. The obvious result is that they often become pregnant, or make others pregnant. This ignorance, impatience, and thoughtlessness is fairly widespread among both men and women.

Solution: Be prepared. Do not hope or expect that your partner will take care of—or even know much about—birth control.

Men: Keep condoms in your room. Silly as it may sound, also keep one in your wallet and a few in your car. Replace unused condoms with new ones after eight or nine months.

Women: *Also* keep condoms in your room, purse, and car—*and* use a second form of birth control as well: The Pill, an IUD, or a diaphragm and spermicidal cream or jelly (together these count as a single form of birth control).

Unfortunately, condoms alone are only about 90% effective in preventing pregnancy. That means that if you and your partner use only condoms for a year, there is a 10% chance that a pregnancy will result. Vaginal contraceptives and diaphragms (even when used with spermicide) are even riskier: They're only about 80% effective. Even an IUD is only about 95% effective.

If you truly want to prevent *pregnancy rather than simply lower the chances of it occurring, use two forms of birth control together.* I strongly recommend condoms plus either an IUD, a cervical cap, or a diaphragm and spermicide. Each of these combinations provides double protection against pregnancy.

Norplant, a new form of birth control, inserted under the skin of a woman's arm, has just been approved by the FDA. It's 99% effective.

The only forms of birth control that are adequately (98% +) effective when used alone are the Pill, Norplant, sterilization, abstinence, and the use of an alternative (or no) orifice.

Condoms, spermicidal creams and jellies, and other vaginal contraceptives are available to anyone at any drugstore. Birth control pills must be prescribed by a doctor; IUDs, cervical caps, Norplant, and diaphragms are also available only through gynecologists and other physicians.

Most universities and liberal arts colleges (except Catholic ones, of course) sell condoms, vaginal contraceptives, and other nonprescription forms of birth control to students at reasonable prices through their campus health clinics. Usually it is also possible to have a doctor at your college clinic prescribe birth control pills or arrange for an IUD or cervical cap. (None of these services, unfortunately, is normally available at community, vocational, technical, business, or junior colleges.)

Being prepared also means saying no to sex when adequate birth control isn't available. Saying no can of course be difficult for both you and your partner; but it's quite a bit less painful than an unwanted and unintended pregnancy. The frustrating but clear-headed truth is that it makes sense to wait to make love until you've got adequate protection.

Be especially wary of the following:

• If your partner says "Don't worry" or "It's been taken care of," or even "You won't get pregnant, I promise." Even though it will break the romantic mood, find out *exactly* what your partner means. His or her idea of what is safe may not actually be very safe at all. It may even be nothing more than empty reassurance.

• If your partner says, "I'm not fertile right now" or "I can't get pregnant now" or "It's the wrong time of the month." Plenty of women get pregnant every year because they believed they were making love at a "safe" time. *Timing is not an adequate substitute for birth control.*

• Rhythm, withdrawal, astrological birth control, yogic birth control, or desperate hopes. Don't fool yourself, or anyone else: None of these methods works.

• The passion of the moment. "I was swept away," "I couldn't help myself," and "I wanted him/her so badly" all often lead to pregnancy. *Restrain yourself* for the moment. First get adequate birth control; *then* get swept away.

A major portion of college rapes are committed by a friend or acquaintance of the victim.

Many campus rapes are "date rapes": A woman and man go on a date together, end up somewhere alone, and perhaps kiss and fondle. At some point the woman says, "That's enough" or "No more," but the man ignores her wishes and eventually has sex with her by force.

Far less common, but at least as awful, are rapes that occur when a woman is too drunk or drugged to defend herself. These rapes often take place at parties. Sometimes more than one man is involved, and usually most or all of them know the victim.

Solutions for women:

Solution 1: Do not expect that date rape (or any other kind of rape) cannot happen to you. Just as college campuses (even the sleepiest and most rural ones) are not always safe, not all college students are safe to be with. Never assume from the start that anyone (including the minister's son—and, for that matter, the minister) is trustworthy, compassionate, and considerate. Let him demonstrate his caring and trustworthiness over time. Get to know someone—and let your attraction to him build—slowly and steadily. Don't forget that strangers can be dangerous.

Solution 2: Be very clear about what you want or don't want. Men often believe (or claim) that women have led them on or misled them, and that they have a right to any sex they've been "promised." Daffy as this idea may be, if you are less than clear and straightforward, you may unwittingly encourage it. When necessary, say in advance, "I'm not going to sleep with you tonight [or now, or whenever]." Continue to clearly state what you want and do not want, no matter how much the man may whine, wheedle, coax, or accuse. When you need to, tell your friend or date to stop; if he doesn't, repeat yourself loudly and firmly. If necessary, tell him to leave; if he doesn't, call the police.

Remember, too, that you have the right to change your mind during the course of a date, party, or evening about having sex. However, you also have an obligation to clearly state what you want and do not want.

A significant portion of campus rapes are perpetrated by fraternity members, by college athletes and/or at frat parties. The great majority of athletes and fraternity men are sane and reasonable human beings, of course. However, I suggest being a little extra careful at fraternity parties, or when going out with athletes or fraternity men.

Solution 3: Protect yourself. Carry a whistle at all times; blow it whenever you encounter trouble. In tough neighborhoods you may want to carry Mace as well. Avoid walking alone at night. Make use of campus escort services. See pages 184–185 for more details on protecting yourself.

If you *are* raped, get to a hospital as soon as possible afterward. Also call the police to report the incident.

Solutions for men:

Solution 1: Don't rush to have sex. Get to know, trust, and appreciate someone slowly and steadily. Let the relationship, and the emotional and sexual attraction, build gradually. As necessary, restrain yourself for a while.

Solution 2: If a woman seems to be deliberately leading you on, only to run off when you're most aroused, or if she seems to be more interested in your money than you, stop seeing her. She has little or nothing to offer you. Look instead for someone who can genuinely care about you and appreciate you.

Solution 3: Never forget these three simple facts:

(1) No friend or date ever owes you sex.

(2) If a woman clearly says no to sex and you have sex with her forcibly, that's rape—even if she's your date or girlfriend (or wife), and even if she has led you on.

(3) For committing rape, you can go to jail for decades.

Potential sexual partners who have sexually transmitted diseases won't always tell you that they have them.

Keeping silent is cruel, selfish, and, in the case of AIDS, potentially fatal. Yet college students do sometimes keep their illnesses a secret—until it is too late.

Solution 1: Before you have sex with anyone, very clearly and specifically ask if he or she has any disease you should know about. If you do not get an equally clear and specific answer, insist on one. ("Don't worry about it" or "Everything will be fine" are not clear, specific answers.) If you still do not get a clear answer, *do not take any chances.* At the very least, follow solution 2 below. But also think seriously about getting away from this person—he or she apparently wants to keep important information from you, and does not seem to care if you contract his or her illness.

None of this means that you shouldn't make love with someone who does have a sexually transmitted disease. *In general,* condoms will prevent you from catching or giving anyone any such illness. But you must first learn exactly what disease the other person has, so that you can decide how to proceed (or not to proceed). If your potential partner does have a sexually transmitted disease, I *strongly* urge the two of you to consult with a doctor before making love; he can provide you with complete information on protection, prevention, and cures.

Solution 2: If you are a man, always wear a condom. If you are a woman, insist that your partner always wear a condom. You can dispense with the condoms when *all* of these five conditions have been fulfilled: (1) you have built a steady and ongoing relationship; (2) your partner assures you that he or she has no sexually transmittable illness; (3) your partner isn't having sex with anyone else and agrees to remain monogamous; (4) you believe you can trust your partner, and (5) you do not need condoms for adequate birth control (i.e., one of you is sterile or is taking the Pill).

17

What You'll Learn in College

Many of the important skills you'll need for your future career won't be taught in college. Neither will many of the important skills you'll need for everyday life as an adult.

Much of what you'll learn in college—how to make intelligent choices, how to care for both yourself and others, how to say no effectively, and so on—won't be taught in any classes. You'll learn them on your own, both in college and outside of it, through experience, trial and error, and interaction with others.

Solution 1: Since you can't learn everything you need in the classroom, seek it elsewhere. And why not arrange to get academic credit for it as well?

Here are some possibilities:

(1) Do one or more independent studies. Independent study enables you to focus on subjects and topics that most intrigue you, while building your intuitive, analytical, and research skills.

(2) Do one or more internships. An internship is the single best way to prepare yourself for any career, and to find out what a particular field, job, or organization is like. It also gives you hands-on working experience in a field or organization that interests you. This experience will look great on a résumé, and will help you to get a full-time job in the field after you graduate. Internships can also provide you with valuable contacts, referrals, and inside information. Most

197

colleges award academic credit for internships, and some internships pay a salary as well. For more details on this subject, see pages 129–130.

(3) Work as a volunteer in a public service organization. Some colleges give academic credit for volunteer work; if yours doesn't, you may still be able to get credit for it by calling your work an internship or an independent study.

(4) Take a practicum and/or a fieldwork course. These are courses that require you to be out in the real world, working with people—not just with concepts and theories.

(5) Spend a term or a year in an off-campus program, ideally one in another culture or country. Most colleges have a variety of such programs available. The most common program is often called Junior Year Abroad, and involves studying for one academic year or term at a campus in another country. Your college catalog will list some or all of its off-campus study options. Many schools also have an off-campus study office or coordinator.

If none of your school's standard off-campus study options appeals to you, you can hand-tailor your own program by taking a leave of absence and enrolling as a nondegree student at another institution of your choice. Be sure to check with your registration office in advance to make sure that the study you have planned will be accepted for transfer credit.

Solution 2: Whenever you may need something—information, assistance, guidance, support, instruction, or advice—*ask for it.* Your opportunities for learning are not limited to the items listed in your college's catalog. The most valuable and important learning skill of all may be knowing what to ask and who to ask it of.

Get used to asking teachers, parents, administrators, friends, and anyone else for whatever information or instruction you may need. This is what networking is all about. It's also what philosophy, education, and growth are all about.

Much of what you'll learn in college will be trivial, irrelevant or self-evident.

Indeed, some instructors and textbooks go so far as to make what is simple or obvious sound complicated and intellectual, usually by couching it in highfalutin language. Some belabor the obvious; others attempt to refute the obvious.

Solution: The best way to avoid the trivial and the irrelevant is to seek out the best instructors and pursue the subjects, courses, and other educational activities that most interest you. The more you intelligently exercise your freedom of choice, the more useful and meaningful your college education will be.

Furthermore, the more choices you have in the first place, the more relevant your education will be. Therefore, consider attending a college that has few specific graduation requirements and/or one that permits you to design your own academic program.

Some of what you'll be taught in college will be debatable. Some will later be disproved and discredited. Some will simply be false.

As we human beings grope toward new insight and knowledge, we naturally discover that what once appeared to be true or absolute is no longer so irrefutable or one-sided.

Perhaps the most important thing you'll learn in college is that much of what people believed to be true in the past no longer seems true today. By implication, much of what we believe today to be true will sooner or later be proven to be incomplete, inaccurate, or incorrect.

Solution: Take everything you learn—both in college and elsewhere—with a grain (and sometimes much more than a grain) of salt. As a famous Zen master once said, faith and doubt are both necessary for true insight.

Some of what you'll learn in college may contradict what you learned in high school.

In general, college instructors are far more knowledgeable than high school teachers. Often they're a good deal more open-minded and intelligent as well.

Indeed, many of us college teachers spend a significant portion of our time helping students to unlearn some of the nonsense they acquired in high school.

Solution: When something you learn in college conflicts with something you learned in high school, believe your college instructor or textbook. Ninety percent of the time the information you learned in high school will be incorrect.

Still, it is an excellent idea to discuss any apparent contradiction with your instructor. Follow the process for resolving contradictions described on page 123.

18

The Value of Your Education (and Your Degree)

Your academic preparation and study in a subject may not completely prepare you for a job in that field.

Academic study provides only some of the knowledge and skills you'll need to do well in the job, career, or organization of your choice. You will also need intelligence, patience, and a willingness to work reasonably hard. Practical knowledge, hands-on experience, and/or the right contacts may also be required.

Solution: Don't expect your coursework and your degree to get you the ideal job. Supplement your regular study with the following:

An internship. Get yourself some practical experience in or with the job, field, or organization that most interests you while you're still in college. You'll graduate not only with useful experience under your belt, but with some useful contacts, a solid and varied understanding of the field, and maybe even a job offer.

If possible, do two or three internships before you graduate; the more experience you can get, the better. For more details on internships, see pages 129–130.

Volunteer work. If you plan to work in public or social service, or any other nonprofit field, spend some time as a volunteer. See page 162 for more information.

Informational interviews. During your last year of school, call up some organizations that interest you and arrange a few interviews. These will give you current inside information on the field, and they may sometimes lead to a job offer as well.

Summer jobs. If you will not be taking classes in the summer, try to spend each summer working in the organization or general field that you hope to work in once you graduate. You'll almost certainly have to take a low-level (and perhaps menial) job, but the connection with the organization or field may nevertheless prove invaluable. You'll learn some inside information, and you'll have established some important ties that you may be able to build on later.

A bachelor's degree is currently required for virtually all white-collar jobs—but this degree alone won't make you employable, no matter what your major is in.

All degrees, from associates' to doctorates, are minimum credentials. Taken alone, they will not get you jobs, or even job interviews. Degrees are often necessities, but they are rarely door-openers.

Employers typically use degrees to make a kind of first cut. Job applicants without the required degree(s) are immediately rejected; those with them are then evaluated, and the best of the bunch are called in for interviews.

Solution: Consider carefully what you want to do for a living. Do some internships and/or volunteer work. Go on several informational interviews. Work in the appropriate field or organization during summers.

When the time comes to apply for jobs, write the best basic résumé that you can. Amend your résumé for each job you apply for, so that you look as close to ideally suited for that job as possible. Don't just answer ads; network with others to find those jobs that never get advertised.

Job-hunt thoroughly and vigorously—in fact, once you've graduated, consider job-hunting your full-time occupation. Be patient and keep trying; expect rejection the great majority of the time. When you land one of the jobs you want, celebrate.

For excellent information on job-hunting and career exploration, see Richard Nelson Bolles's *What Color Is Your Parachute?* (Ten Speed

Press, 1991); for good advice on résumé writing, see Richard Lathrop's *Who's Hiring Who?* (Ten Speed Press, 1989).

Many jobs absolutely require a bachelor's or master's degree, regardless of your other qualifications. Strangely enough, this degree need not always be in an appropriate field. A social service agency, for example, might hire someone with a master's degree in history or engineering and little experience, yet refuse to even interview an applicant with a B.A. in a social service field and three years of experience. An advertising agency might require that each of its writers have a bachelor's degree, although the degree may be in any field: physical education, Buddhist studies, nursing, etc.

This approach to hiring is clearly insane, but it's also quite widespread (though, fortunately, not universal).

The simple-minded rationale behind this approach goes like this: Anyone with a bachelor's degree must be smarter and more capable than anyone without one, and anyone with a master's degree must be smarter and more capable than anyone with just a bachelor's degree.

Even on the surface, this approach is absurd. But many employers embrace it for one significant reason: It makes hiring simpler and more quantifiable. (It also makes hiring less effective.)

At present, a graduate degree is now required for about one-third to one-half of all white-collar jobs. This percentage will almost certainly increase over the next decade.

Solution 1: Once you know what field you want to work in, find out what degree(s) you'll need to get and keep the job you desire. You can get this information from your instructors, from the people you work for and with in your internships, and from the people who grant you informational interviews.

Then plan to complete any necessary degrees—even if doing so seems absurd and irrelevant, and you're getting the degrees simply as credentials.

Do *not* bypass getting the correct degree in the hope that your great intelligence and/or enthusiasm will compensate, because from the perspective of potential employers, they won't. Remember, most employers check *first* to see if you have the right degree; if you don't, they won't even bother to consider your intelligence or enthusiasm.

If a graduate degree is necessary, keep in mind that applications may be due as early as January 1 for the following fall; be sure to apply for any appropriate assistantships, fellowships, and/or other forms of financial assistance.

Also keep in mind that graduate and professional programs in any field can differ quite widely from one college or university to the next. Research schools and programs carefully, just as you did for your undergraduate education. Consider each program's overall approach, its graduation requirements, the available financial aid, and the location of each school. Visit those schools that interest you most; sit in on a few classes, and talk with some of the instructors and students in the program.

A wide range of unusual master's degree programs are now available in many fields. These include evening, weekend, and once-a-month programs; low-residence and nonresidence programs; and design-your-own programs. Consult John Bear's books, *Bear's Guide to Earning Non-Traditional Degrees* (Ten Speed Press, 1988) and *College Degrees By Mail* (Ten Speed Press, 1990) for details on many of these programs.

In recent years, quite a few schools have developed Master of Arts in Humanities and Master of Arts in Liberal Studies programs. These are highly flexible programs designed for people who want or need master's degrees, but who do not need to earn those degrees in particular fields. In most of these programs, the primary requirements are to take six to ten courses of your choice, and perhaps complete a final project.

Solution 2: If you have the skills and experience to do a job well but have a degree in a different field, apply for the job anyway. Since many employers will seriously consider your application if you have the right *level* of degree, even if that degree is in an unrelated field, you may be granted an interview. Be sure to emphasize your appropriate skills and experience in your cover letter.

Solution 3: If you have the skills and experience to do a job well, but don't have the level of degree that the employer asks for, feel free to make your best case for yourself in your letter of application. Understand, however, that your chances of getting an interview are about five percent.

A college education will not necessarily transform you into an informed, articulate, well-rounded citizen capable of thinking clearly and making wise decisions.

At age thirty-six, after over a decade of college teaching, I still don't have any idea what "well-rounded" means, although college catalogs persist in using the term. As for the rest, college will help somewhat, but most of the responsibility for your intellectual and emotional growth is—and always will be—your own.

Solution: Education and growth don't—and shouldn't—stop after you graduate from college. Becoming and staying informed, articulate, and clearheaded is an ongoing task that requires regular (but well-rewarded) effort.

Continue to acquire, examine, consider, challenge, and question information. Read; discuss and debate important topics with others; ponder; meditate; test out your ideas; and come to your own conclusions. You will slowly but steadily grow in wisdom.

19

Staying Sane

**College will sometimes make impossible or contradictory demands
on you and your time.**

This sort of situation will arise throughout your college career. For
example, your literature teacher expects you to lead the class during
precisely the same two hours as your girlfriend's birthday party;
you're put into a three-person research group with two football
players, both of whom have no intention of doing any research; or
major papers are coincidentally due in all four of your classes on the
same day—the day after your parents will come to visit you from two
thousand miles away.

The most difficult times, not surprisingly, are shortly before
midterm and final exams, when you may find yourself with more
"absolutely necessary" studying and preparation than you have time
for.

Solution 1: Explain your situation openly to the people involved,
and ask for their help. Sometimes this may mean asking a teacher to
extend a deadline or reschedule a project, duty, or event; sometimes it
may mean saying, "That's the bind I'm in; can you suggest a
solution?"; and sometimes it may simply mean asking the other
person to understand your dilemma and take it into consideration.

Most teachers—and most other people, too—are perfectly willing
to be flexible about dates, deadlines, and assignments when difficult
or unusual circumstances arise. You don't need a full-blown crisis (an
imaginary dead uncle, a life-threatening illness, etc.) to get them to
bend their rules, let you off a hook, or otherwise be of help.

The best course is to be simple and straightforward about what you need and why you need it. For example, "I've got a big chemistry test on the same day this paper is due; could I turn it in on the fifteenth instead of the tenth?" Or, "My boyfriend is going in for eye surgery tomorrow and he's asked me to be there with him; may I lead the class discussion next week instead?" Most people are perfectly willing to make changes and exceptions for good reason. And even those that aren't willing are usually more sympathetic once they understand what's going on.

Never be afraid to ask for what you want or need. You can't really lose—after all, the worst answer you can possibly get is no.

If you genuinely need to ask the same person to make an exception two or even three times during the same term, that's okay. You haven't somehow used up your right to ask for help by making an earlier request.

Solution 2: As much as possible, pace yourself throughout the term, so that you don't get overwhelmed with work—except before midterms and finals, of course, when being overwhelmed is usually a fact of life. Try to stay on top of all your studying and class preparation; schedule your day and week so that you can squeeze everything in, including sufficient leisure time. When a major project is due or an exam is coming up, try to leave enough time for it without having to ignore the rest of your courses (or the rest of your life).

I find that it helps to make up a general plan for the day in the morning, and a general plan for the upcoming week during the weekend before. I actually make written lists, and break them down into things that absolutely must be done and things that I hope to do. It is not necessary to follow these lists to the letter, of course—and certainly do not let them run your life.

I also find it very useful to keep a datebook, in which I note down upcoming classes, tests, appointments, events, obligations, and due dates for projects. Most college bookstores and office supply shops carry a selection of inexpensive datebooks costing three to eight dollars. (Much more expensive ones are available, but they're just ripoffs for gullible yuppies.)

If you find this whole list-making and datebook-keeping approach too anal or compulsive, ignore it.

Solution 3: When you simply do not have the time to do everything you have to, don't do one thing thoroughly and the others badly or not at all. Instead, put at least some effort into everything. If you don't have time to study for all of your courses, do most of the studying for each; if necessary, skim rather than read less-than-essential material. You are usually better off doing passably well in all your courses than extremely well in one and poorly in the rest.

If you must cut corners on your class preparation, try to catch up again as quickly as possible.

Solution 4: If you find yourself chronically overwhelmed, or repeatedly unable to keep up with everything in your life, you are almost certainly asking and expecting too much of yourself. *Stop trying to do the impossible.* You may need to do one or more of the following:

• Drop one or more classes, and/or take fewer classes in future terms. (Dropping classes in the middle of the term can sometimes affect your financial aid status, so check with your financial aid office first.)

• Quit your job, or work fewer hours per week at it. If necessary, find a less stressful or time-consuming job.

• Cut back or eliminate some of your campus, church, or other volunteer activities (e.g., serving on a committee, working on the student newspaper, planning sorority events, etc.). These can eat up enormous amounts of time, and it's very easy to commit yourself to more than you can handle. (Most students make these commitments at the beginning of the term; when the first real crunch hits a few weeks later, they find themselves in a bind.)

It's important to keep a perspective on these activities. Remember that they are usually far less important than your studies, your job, and your personal relationships. Be very selective in the clubs you join and the activities you volunteer for. If you get in over your head, get right back out again, explaining politely that your studies, job, and/or personal life simply don't leave you with sufficient time. People will almost always understand and empathize—and if they don't, that's their problem, not yours.

• If absolutely necessary, take an incomplete in one (but no more than one) of your classes. I recommend this only when no other decent option is available, because incompletes can be dangerous. Read my warnings about incompletes on pages 150–151 carefully. If you do take an incomplete, it is imperative that you complete the course before the next term begins.

Solution 5: Understand that these situations are sometimes just plain unavoidable, and that there may be no good solution. Nevertheless, you *do* have choices, and it is up to you to make the best (or least harmful) one that you can.

When you're in a tight spot and there seems to be no ideal or easy way out, don't blame yourself for not being able to come up with a wonderful, magic solution. Instead, make a mental or written list of all your options; note the probable pros and cons of each; then make the best decision you can, reminding yourself that every one of your options will result in some problem or pain.

Sometimes college will seem pointless, irrelevant, or just plain ridiculous.

There's a good reason for this: Some of what goes on in college, including some of what you will be required to learn, is pointless, irrelevant, or ridiculous. Because of conflicting interests, battles over money and organizational turf, interpersonal friction, and people's desire for power and control, colleges end up giving students an education that is less relevant and appropriate than it should be.

But these problems aren't unique to colleges. All organizations designed by human beings, no matter how altruistic, well-intentioned, or genuinely helpful they may be, are partly pointless, irrelevant, or ridiculous. Virtually no organization on earth is as efficient, sane, and humane as it can and should be.

Solution 1: Take your own intellectual and emotional growth very seriously—but take your college education somewhat less seriously. Understand that some of what goes on will be dopey or absurd; also understand that some of what will go on in any organization you work for or belong to, either now or in the future, will be equally dopey and absurd.

At those times when the dopiness and absurdity reach a peak, remind yourself that events tend to work in cycles, and that things will probably settle down again soon. In the meantime, stay as sane, as calm, and as separate from the craziness as you can.

Also remind yourself that you are in school partly to earn a practical credential: a college degree. When college seems pointless and irrelevant in all other ways, remember that you still have this one highly pragmatic reason to stay in school.

Solution 2: Take a term or a year off to work, travel, or study elsewhere. Look into off-campus programs sponsored by your college. Get out of your current environment and find a different one.

At best, you'll find something you want to do more. At worst, you'll discover that your college wasn't so bad after all—and you'll be able to return with lowered expectations, less disappointment, and more patience.

For all of these options, except an off-campus study program sponsored by your college, you will need to take an official leave of absence. At most colleges, you can do this simply by filling out a form. Contact your registration office for details. If you plan to take courses elsewhere, arrange in advance to have the credits transferred in; see page 79 for details.

Taking a leave of absence may affect certain forms of financial aid; check with your financial aid office for detailed information.

Solution 3: If your college becomes simply intolerable, you may be at the wrong school. Consider transferring to one more suited to your goals, needs, and personality. Remember to research colleges thoroughly and carefully, and to visit those schools that most interest you. Meanwhile, grit your teeth and finish the current term where you are.

Solution 4: If college in general seems wrong for you, it may be best to stop being a student, at least for a while. But don't just drop out. First, finish up the current term if you can, so that you can leave in good academic standing and get some more credits under your belt. Then apply for a one-year leave of absence through your registration office. This allows you to later reenroll without having to reapply to the college. At the same time, it obligates you to nothing: You can choose to never come back, transfer elsewhere, or come back before the year is up (just notify the registration office a month or so before the term begins). If, when your leave of absence is over, you wish to extend it or withdraw from the college, just let the registration office know in a letter.

College creates a great deal of stress.

There's no getting around it: College is frequently a high-stress environment. This stress can be coped with, and even reduced, but it cannot be done away with or avoided completely.

Part of the problem is the time commitment involved: The average full-time course load of fifteen credits requires thirty to forty-five hours of academic work per week, including class time. Just before midterm and final exams, this commitment goes up dramatically, to fifty to seventy hours.

Solution 1: Limit the stress as much as possible through one or more of these methods (some of which I have discussed in detail earlier):

• Take a reduced course load. You can take as few as twelve credits at most schools and still be considered a full-time student for financial aid and registration purposes.

• Become a part-time student.

• Live off-campus, where things are less frazzled and frantic, especially during the middle and end of the term.

• Limit the number of hours you spend at your job. Or quit your job entirely (if you can afford to).

• Limit the number of hours you spend in organized extracurricular activities (volunteer work, campus clubs and organizations, etc.).

Solution 2: Cope with the remaining stress by doing some or all of the following:

• Exercise regularly. This can help enormously. Pick an exercise you *enjoy,* regardless of what kind of strength or endurance it builds. Walking, bicycling, swimming, and yoga are as good at reducing stress as running, weightlifting, and competitive sports.

• Get enough sleep. Students often don't.

• Eat well. You do not have to live on tofu and bean sprouts, nor do you have to eat foods from all the different food groups. Do, however, limit your intake of junk food and fast food, both of which tend to be high in calories and low in nutrition.

Sugar and caffeine (found in most soft drinks as well as in coffee and tea) can actually heighten stress; so can alcohol in some cases. Eat and drink all of these in moderation; when you're under stress, it's often best to strictly limit them or avoid them entirely.

• Meditate. Meditation does wonders for reducing anxiety and stress, and it also tends to promote physical health and emotional stability. Sometimes it increases people's intellectual and spiritual insight as well.

There are dozens of different styles of meditation; Zen meditation (zazen) and transcendental meditation (TM) are the most popular. I recommend Zen meditation (which I have practiced for years) because it takes less than ten minutes to learn and does not require you to adopt any beliefs, traditions, rituals, or other practices. You can, of course, develop your own style of meditation.

A list of many of the meditation centers and groups in North America appears in Ram Dass's book *Journey of Awakening* (Bantam, 1990). Simple, straightforward instructions on how to do Zen meditation appear in *The Three Pillars of Zen* by Philip Kapleau (Doubleday, 1989).

• Talk things over with others. "Others" can be friends, teachers, a psychologist, a minister or rabbi, your parents, or anyone else whom you trust and who will truly and openly listen to you. This can be a surprisingly effective—and surprisingly easy—stress reducer.

Most colleges (except for vocational, technical, and business schools) have at least one psychologist on staff who is available to students at no charge, by appointment. Most universities and liberal arts colleges also employ campus ministers, who make themselves very available for counseling. Usually there is at least one Catholic priest, one Protestant minister, and one rabbi on staff.

People *not* to talk things over with are: Those who have an answer for everything, those who give knee-jerk advice, and those who are too self-involved to genuinely hear what you have to say.

• Pray. This works for a great many people, including many nonreligious ones.

During midterm weeks and the last two weeks of each term, most of your fellow students, and some of your teachers, will be grouchy, frantic, exhausted, and/or wired. You may be as well.

Everyone gets stressed out by exams and major papers—including teachers, who have to prepare and grade the exams, and read and grade the papers. Particularly at the end of the term, everyone's patience starts to wear thin around the edges.

Solution: Try not to make any major life decisions during these times; your judgment may be skewed, both by your own stress and by all the frazzled energy in the air. Don't expect too much of other students at these times, either: They're more likely than usual to disappoint you or act weird. Be as patient with yourself and others as you can. If people act short-tempered, irritable, or irrational, cut them some slack.

Meanwhile, cope with the stress by employing some of the techniques described above. And if you live away from home, do *not* let your parents visit until the Hell Weeks are over.

College can be lonely.

Actually, just about any place—including a crowd or your own home—can be lonely at times. Indeed, life itself can sometimes be lonely.

There seem to be three kinds of loneliness:

(1) Circumstantial loneliness, in which you don't have the type or amount of contact with others that you want or need.

(2) Emotional loneliness, in which you feel a strong craving for love, intimacy, or something more undefined.

(3) Existential loneliness, in which you feel that you are irrevocably separate from other beings, and/or from God.

It's of course possible to experience two or all three of these at once. Homesickness, for instance, seems to be a combination of the first two types of loneliness.

I believe that each type of loneliness has its own solution.

Solution 1: Dealing with circumstantial loneliness is the easiest. Get out and meet people. Go to meetings, poetry readings, plays, dances, and other social events. If you have no one to go with, don't be afraid to go on your own. Use the telephone; talk to old and new friends, parents, and anyone else you're already close to.

If you're shy, or afraid of going places or meeting new people, let yourself feel shy and afraid, but go anyway. Take the initiative and introduce yourself to others; most people will appreciate your assertiveness, since most are shy themselves.

Shyness and a fear of meeting new people are extremely common problems—so common that psychological counselors have developed a variety of simple and effective methods for dealing with them. If you have trouble overcoming your fear or shyness on your own, make an appointment with your college's psychologist; explain your problem to him and say that you'd like to learn to become more outgoing and less afraid. He should be able to give you some practical advice and guidance.

Solution 2: Emotional loneliness usually requires a different approach. Much of the solution involves learning to feel good about yourself, appreciate yourself, and enjoy your own company. Paradoxically, this appreciation of yourself tends to lead to better and more fulfilling relationships with others, and to a fuller and happier life in general.

Chronic loneliness often has its roots in a dysfunctional family—a family in which the parents were not sufficiently fair, honest, or loving with their children. Children of dysfunctional families often feel lonely and isolated from others.

Talking with a psychological counselor can often help enormously. If you prefer not to see a counselor (and even if you do see one), I strongly recommend reading David D. Burn's excellent book on overcoming loneliness, *Intimate Connections* (Morrow, 1985 and New American Library, 1985). Burn's book is simple, practical, and very effective.

Many thousands of people have also found a solution through Adult Children Anonymous (commonly known as ACA), a program and support group for children of dysfunctional families. ACA is a spinoff of Alcoholics Anonymous—indeed, some ACA groups call themselves Adult Children of Alcoholics (ACOA)—but the program is intended for anyone who grew up in a dysfunctional family, not just the children of alcoholics. ACA groups cost nothing to attend (a donation is optional), and they can often do more to help heal loneliness and other pain than traditional counseling. Many people find that it's tremendously healing and relieving simply to find people who feel the same way or have similar backgrounds.

Most ACA groups meet once a week; you may attend as often or as infrequently as you wish. Virtually every large city has at least one ACA group; many small and midsize towns have them as well. If Adult Children Anonymous or Adult Children of Alcoholics is not listed in your local phone directory, check with one or more of the following to locate the nearest ACA group:

- the local chapter of Alcoholics Anonymous
- the local chapter of Al-Anon
- First Call For Help

Solution 3: Existential loneliness is a very different matter. Writers, thinkers, philosophers, psychologists, and theologians have been dealing with the problem for centuries, and they've come up with a variety of solutions and nonsolutions. The number of books that deal with the topic is enormous, but some writers you might begin with are Alan Watts, Erich Fromm, Rollo May, Paul Tillich, and Abraham Maslow.

I also urge you to talk with some of your instructors in philosophy, religion, psychology, and/or sociology. Ask them to recommend some appropriate reading; if you like, ask them for their own opinions and ideas on the subject. Feel free to approach any instructor during her office hours, even if you're not taking one of her classes; part of every teacher's job is to respond to sincere inquiries from students, and many will be happy to help you.

Priests, ministers, and rabbis can also be extremely helpful, both in offering insight and suggesting books to read. Feel free to approach not only your own clergyperson but any of your campus ministers—or, indeed, any spiritual leader whom you think may offer you some useful insight.

If your college is in a small town, there may be little or nothing to do.

This can be particularly true if you attend a small college, which may offer few on-campus social events and activities.

A lack of stimulation can often have a cumulative effect. It might not be much of a problem during your first year, but it begins to bother you in your second—and by your third you feel that your head may explode from boredom.

Solution 1: Get away frequently. Don't mope around because there's nothing to do; get in your car and drive to a place where there *is* something going on, such as the nearest big city or large university. If you don't have a car, use public transportation. Or, find an equally bored friend who has a car, and take off together.

Solution 2: If nothing interesting is happening at your college, start something yourself. Throw a major party in your dorm. Start a campus club based on an activity that interests you. Organize a poetry reading series, or a weekly square dance, or anything else you please.

Solution 3: Spend a year or more away from campus.

Most colleges offer at least one or two off-campus programs. Some of these involve spending a term or a year at another college or university, usually in Europe or elsewhere overseas; other programs are based on fieldwork at marine biology stations, archaeological digs, forest preserves, etc. Some of these programs are called Junior Year Abroad; often they are open to sophomores and seniors as well as juniors. Check your college catalog or call your registration office for information on the off-campus programs your college offers.

You can also arrange your own off-campus program, of course. Pick a college or university where you would like to study for a term, or a year, or up to two years; apply to take courses there as a nondegree student, and arrange to take a leave of absence from your home school (see page 209 for details on how). Make sure to get advance approval for the courses you plan to transfer in; follow the instructions on page 79.

Another option is to take time off to work or travel. The drawback to this, however, is that when you return to college, you won't be any closer to graduation, and you'll have to spend your remaining terms in the same boring place.

Taking a leave of absence may affect certain forms of financial aid, so be sure to check this out with your financial aid office.

Solution 4: If you absolutely cannot stand another term in the boondocks, consider transferring to another school.

You may go through a major slump in your second or third year. This is neither inevitable nor as awful as it may sound.

About half of all students find themselves bored with, tired of, or unenthusiastic about college sometime during their sophomore and/

or junior years. Typically, they lose their energy and excitement for college (and perhaps for learning in general). They feel as if they're just going through the motions of taking courses, doing the work, and earning credits.

In part, this kind of response can occur when you've done *anything* for a couple of years in a row. In part it occurs when students realize that college is less interesting and sane than they had expected.

Solution 1: If you follow the advice in the previous chapters (especially chapters 1, 7, and 9) and pick your college, classes, and instructors carefully, you are far less likely to become bored and dissatisfied. And if you choose to solve problems rather than let them overwhelm you, you are much more likely to stay reasonably happy and energized throughout your college career.

If you find yourself in a slump, however, use some of these techniques discussed earlier:

- Get away from campus frequently.

- Spend a term, a year, or more away from campus—traveling, working, or studying elsewhere.

- Vary your intellectual diet. Sign up for some unusual courses— ones that sound challenging but intriguing. Do an internship or two. Arrange some independent studies.

- If necessary, transfer to another college.

Solution 2: Tell yourself that the slump is temporary, and that your energy and interest will almost certainly return as graduation gets closer (and no longer seems impossibly far away). This isn't just a motivational technique; it's the truth. What may seem like a never-ending case of the blues will almost certainly disappear of its own accord by your senior year, and perhaps well before.

You'll likely go through at least one major emotional crisis during your college years.

This is perfectly normal and natural. In fact, most people go through several major emotional crises in their lives—and end up stronger and wiser because of them.

Personal crises are not terrifying events to be avoided, but important opportunities for growth. Each crisis represents a conflict of values, beliefs, or principles—a conflict that requires resolution, ideally in favor of what is sanest and most humane.

By the time many people reach middle age, they realize from experience that these conflicts are both helpful and instructive. As a result, they no longer seem so threatening or painful.

But for many college students, who may not have had any (or many) such upheavals before, an emotional crisis may seem horrible and devastating.

Solution: The pain of your crisis is very real, but it is temporary. Instead of running away from the pain, make your best efforts to understand the issues that underlie it. This may itself be painful, but the result will almost always be understanding, wisdom, and faster relief. As much as possible, talk things out honestly with the people involved. Ask the advice of others you trust. If you like, bring the matter up with a campus psychologist or minister.

To resolve the crisis, you will almost certainly have to make a choice or decision. Don't put this off unnecessarily; failing to act or choose is itself a choice and an action. Look at the circumstances as clearly as you can, and make the wisest decision you are capable of. Then accept the consequences of that decision, and learn what you can from it.

Throughout the crisis, try to stay as calm and as clearheaded as possible. Use the tips on pages 210–211 to help manage your stress and anxiety.

Lastly, remind yourself that at some point relatively soon the crisis will be resolved, and your life will be less bumpy once again—and, very likely, better because of the decision you made.

Many students get very anxious during their senior year.

Who wouldn't be anxious about going out on his own, finding the right job, locating a decent place to live, leaving familiar friends and a familiar environment, and beginning to build a life for himself?

Solution: Go ahead and be anxious. Your anxiety is real and appropriate.

Remind yourself, however, that a great many college graduates before you (and a great many nongraduates, too) have managed to build happy, successful careers and lives for themselves. The world contains at least as many opportunities as it does obstacles, and with intelligence and patience, you should be able to make a place for yourself in it.

In the meantime, use some of the stressbusters on pages 210–211 to help make your day-to-day life more sane and serene.

If your anxiety nevertheless becomes so large that it begins to paralyze you or take control of your life, visit a campus psychologist. He'll be quite familiar with your situation, and he should be able to offer you some good advice and some practical methods for reducing your anxiety.

20

The Pleasures and Rewards of College

Most colleges will cause you only a small percentage of the problems described in the previous nineteen chapters.

Throughout this book I've pointed out the potential problems and hazards of college. In this chapter I'd like to focus on the many positive things that ultimately make most North American colleges and universities good places to be.

All of the problems described in the first nineteen chapters of this book are real. Some of them are quite common. But not all of them are going to come your way as a college student; in fact, perhaps only about one in five will affect you directly.

Each different college has its own strengths and weaknesses, just as you have your own strengths and weaknesses as a student. Each school has its own unique combination of incompetence, mismanagement, and weirdness; each also has its own array of first-rate people, policies, and facilities. No one college has all—or even most—of the problems described in this book.

Despite their problems, most colleges are worthwhile places to be.

If they weren't, I wouldn't be warning you about their potential hazards; instead, I'd be advising you not to attend college at all.

For most students, college is a largely—and often over-whelmingly—positive experience. It's true that colleges, like other institutions created by human beings, often are not what they could or should be. But it's also true that, overall, most colleges and universities manage to succeed in their mission: to help students think, question, learn, and grow.

A few colleges, perhaps one out of sixty, are almost uniformly awful. But ninety-eight percent of North American colleges and universities have some extremely worthwhile things to offer. Your job as a student is to seek them out and make good use of them.

Most teachers, administrators, and staff people genuinely do want to help you.

Without this general concern for students, their education, and their well-being, colleges would be worthless.

Four-fifths of the people who work for colleges and universities genuinely share a desire to help students. These people may not always be wise or even competent, but they at least have your best interests in mind. This means that in general, you can trust them and turn to them for help—and that's worth a lot.

As for those twenty percent who don't want to be helpful, avoid or ignore them as much as possible. When appropriate, complain about them to their superiors.

College can make you a better thinker, reader, writer, and observer.

Many students go to college expecting little or nothing more than training for a career, a few good parties, and the credential of a degree. Often, though, they end up with all that they expected and a great deal more.

If you're willing to put a reasonable amount of effort and energy into college, it can make you more observant, more informed, more eloquent, and more perceptive. These qualities can be as essential to your professional and social success as they are to your training and your degree.

College can help you become a wiser and happier person.

In fact, if you're willing to put in real thought, concentration, and time—time spent pondering, questioning, analyzing, sometimes disagreeing, and often coming up with your own point of view—then college can help you to become a more aware, intuitive, confident, self-reliant, and, ultimately, successful human being.

College is a good place to meet friends and lovers.

Nowhere else in the world are you as likely to meet so many other people who share at least some of your interests—and who have the time, the inclination, and the lack of commitments to make a personal (and sometimes intimate or long-lasting) connection with you.

A high percentage of married couples and long-time friends first met each other at college. Even people who dropped out of college often say that they made some of their closest and most valuable contacts when they were students.

College can be fun.

Despite all the potential problems and the undeniably hard work, lots of people have a very good time in college. If you use good judgment, follow most of the advice in this book, and don't take things too seriously (but seriously enough that you don't ignore what's important), you can enjoy yourself immensely as a college student.

Your degree is a valuable credential.

While it's true that for most jobs you need more than just a degree, it's just as true that many jobs and careers are virtually inaccessible without that degree. Indeed, without a college degree, your chances of getting a desirable white-collar job are very slim.

So don't undervalue your degree. It's an important stepping-stone to your success. Just because it doesn't guarantee you the job or career you want, that doesn't make it any less valuable or essential.

If you are careful in choosing which courses to take, which instructors to learn from, and which college to attend, you will make the most of college.

At virtually every college, the instructors and the courses range from horrendous to fascinating, with every stop in between. *If* you track down those first-rate instructors and classes, your college years can be some of the best ones of your life. Remember, though, that the good things about college won't all come to you automatically; you have to go out and find them.

It's just as important to go out and find the right college in the first place. If you find the right school, almost everything will—with a little effort on your part—fall into place: good courses, good teachers, a pleasant social life, and an overall feeling of satisfaction. For most students, that right school is out there.

If you follow the advice in this book, your college years can be very positive and happy ones.

Although this book focuses on solving and avoiding problems, problem solving is not its primary purpose.

The main purposes of this book are to help you get the best and most useful education that you can; to enjoy your years as a college student as much as possible; and to become the happiest, savviest, and most successful student—and person—that you can be.

If my book has helped you as much as I want it to—or if a future edition can be improved in some way—I'd like you to let me know. Write me in care of the publisher, Carol Publishing Group, at 600 Madison Avenue, New York, NY 10022.

May you prosper and live happily, both in college and thereafter.

About the Author

Scott Edelstein has been a student at twelve different colleges and universities and has taught at ten, including the University of Minnesota, Oberlin College, Metropolitan State University, the University of Wisconsin at Milwaukee, Lakewood Community College, and several others. He has also been an advisor, a college-level writing tutor, and an intern in the provost's office at Oberlin College.

Edelstein is the author of three previous books about college: *College: A User's Manual* (Bantam, 1985), *Surviving Freshman Composition* (Lyle Stuart, 1988), and *Putting Your Kids Through College* (Consumer Reports Books, 1989). His streetwise, no-nonsense advice for college students has also appeared in several magazines, including *Glamour, Essence,* and *Campus Life.* Over a hundred of his short pieces on a wide range of subjects have been published in magazines such as *Single Parent, Writer's Digest, The Artist's Magazine,* and many others, and he is the author of several practical guides for writers: *The Indispensable Writer's Guide* (HarperCollins, 1989), *The No-Experience-Necessary Writer's Course* (Scarborough House, 1990), *Manuscript Submission* (Writer's Digest Books, 1990), and *The Writer's Book of Checklists* (Writer's Digest Books, 1991).

Edelstein has a B.A. in writing from Oberlin College and an M.A. in English from the University of Wisconsin at Milwaukee. He is currently at work on his dissertation for a Ph.D. in English from the State University of New York at Buffalo. He lives in Minneapolis with his wife, Barbara.